March of America Facsimile Series

Number 48

Clark's Memoir

George Rogers Clark

Clark's Memoir

from English's Conquest of the Country
by George Rogers Clark

ANN ARBOR
UNIVERSITY MICROFILMS, INC.
A Subsidiary of Xerox Corporation

Foreword

Contained in the provisions of the Treaty of Paris, 1783, by which Great Britain recognized American independence, was an agreement that the United States should possess the Northwest Territory. The man principally responsible for achieving American sovereignty over that territory was George Rogers Clark. His skillfully executed campaigns in the Ohio River Valley during the Revolution had already given America a *de facto* control over much of the region. After the war Clark composed a *Memoir*, which described some of his activities during the Revolution. The manuscript, though undated, was probably written around 1791. It was not published until 1896 when W. H. English included it as part of an appendix to volume one of his *Conquest of the Country Northwest of the River Ohio*. Only the relevant section in the appendix of the W. H. English edition is reproduced here.

George Rogers Clark, elder brother of William Clark of the Lewis and Clark Expedition, was deputy surveyor in Kentucky at the outbreak of the American Revolution. The settlers in Kentucky selected him to represent their need for assistance to the Virginia Assembly in 1776. After some haggling, the Virginians agreed to help and sent powder. Clark, commissioned a major, was entrusted with the organization of the militia for defense.

Convinced that the British planned to seize all the land west of the Alleghenies and to attack Virginia from behind, Clark persuaded the Governor of Virginia, Patrick Henry, to support his plan for a counteroffensive in the West. Clark, by now a lieutenant colonel, received authorization to lead a small force to implement his strategy.

He established a military base at the falls of the Ohio in May, 1778, opposite the site of what is today Louisville. This accomplished, he moved farther down the Ohio River, then proceeded overland and surprised and captured Kaskaskia on the Mississippi, July 4, 1778. By a shrewd use of psychology he won over the French inhabitants of the town, who in turn persuaded the French population in Vincennes and in other villages to renounce their allegiance to Great Britain.

The French also helped Clark win over many of the Indians in the region. They "informed the Indians that their old father, the king of France, was come to life again, had joined the big knife, and was mad at them for fighting for the English; that they would advise them to make peace with the Americans as soon as they could." Clark, who believed that "our general conduct with the Indians was wrong," studied the methods employed by the French and the Spaniards to win their friendship. He soon became a master at the art of dealing with them.

Meanwhile the British lieutenant governor at Detroit, Henry Hamilton, in the following winter recaptured Vincennes. Rather than wait for Hamilton to launch a spring offensive, Clark decided on the desperate gamble of an immediate attack against Vincennes. In the dead of winter, and with a small force, half of which was composed of French volunteers, Clark painfully advanced for eighteen days through the flooded Illinois country. On February 25, 1779, Clark's men were rewarded for their suffering by the surrender of the Vincennes garrison. Clark terminates his *Memoir* shortly after the surrender. The *Memoir* does not, therefore, tell of his subsequent engagements with the English and of the frustrations he experienced in his plan to capture Detroit.

A balance to Clark's *Memoir* is the journal kept by Henry Hamilton. John D. Barnhart has edited the journal and provided additional background about Clark in *Henry Hamilton and George Rogers Clark in the American Revolution* (Crawfordsville, Indiana, 1951). More information about Clark's expeditions can be found in T. C. Pease and M. J. Pease, *George Rogers Clark and the Revolution in Illinois, 1763-1787* ([Springfield, Illinois], 1929).

Clark's Memoir

INTRODUCTORY TO CLARK'S MEMOIR.

The memoir which will now be given was the last and longest account written by General Clark of his campaigns against the British posts northwest of the river Ohio, and the events in Kentucky and Virginia connected therewith.

Attention was first called to the memoir by Mr. John B. Dillon, who published lengthy extracts from it in his history of Indiana about the year 1842. These printed extracts have generally been used by subsequent writers, and the memoir is now published in full for the first time.

The author of this work is in possession of the manuscript copy of the memoir from which Mr. Dillon made his extracts, and has carefully compared it with the copy in possession of Colonel Reuben T. Durrett, of Louisville, Kentucky, and partially with the one in the Draper collection in the Wisconsin Historical Society; these being the only copies of the memoir known to be in existence. The last mentioned is claimed to be the original, but, unfortunately, a number of the leaves have been lost. The manuscript copy in possession of the author is headed with a statement that it is " from a MS. memoir of General George Rogers Clark, composed by himself at the united desire of Presidents Jefferson and Madison, in the possession of Professor Bliss, of Louisville, Kentucky." Professor Bliss, about that time, had undertaken to write a history of General Clark, and the memoir had probably come into his possession for that purpose. But he was shot on the street in Louisville, September 26, 1842, by a rival editor of a newspaper, and died from the wound, having written but a few pages of his contemplated history.

It is said that the original manuscript of the memoir was loaned, from time to time, by the Clark family, to several parties for historical purposes. Mann Butler had it in 1833, and either it, or a copy, was at one time in the Kentucky Historical Society, and at another in the possession of Professor Bliss, but it finally drifted into the hands of Lyman C. Draper, who also contemplated writing a history of George Rogers Clark, but died without doing it, and upon his death the memoir passed into the hands of the Wisconsin Historical Society with other historic papers.

The memoir seems to have been in the form of a letter, and the word "Sir" at the beginning indicates that it was, at least, not addressed to Jefferson and Madison jointly, or to more than one person.

From the letter of Mr. Jefferson, already quoted in the introduction to the Mason letter, it would seem reasonable to infer that Clark was writing the memoir in 1791, the date of Mr. Jefferson's letter. That is not conclusive, however, and there is no date on any of the manuscript copies. Neither does the author remember to have seen any statement as to the exact time it was written.

CLARK'S MEMOIR.

Sir—In fulfilling the engagement I am under to you, with respect to the wars of Kentucky, I must commence with the first settlement of the district, which had been but partially explored previous to the year 1773, when a considerable number of surveyors and private adventurers passed generally through it. The first settlement attempted in Kentucky was by Colonel James Harrod, with some few followers, at Harrodstown, in the spring of 1774, but this party made but small progression in building, etc., before they were obliged to abandon the country on account of the war with the Shawanoes. They marched through the wilderness and joined Colonel Lewis's army. At the close of that war they made preparation and again took possession of their town in the spring of 1775.

In the meantime, Colonel Henderson & Company had purchased the country of the Cherokees (the Cherokees had no right to Kentucky), and made an establishment at Boonesborough, opening a land office, etc., but you are too well acquainted with those circumstances to need any information.

It was at this period (1775) that I first had thoughts of paying some attention to the interests of this country (Kentucky). The proprietors, Henderson & Company, took great pains to ingratiate themselves in the favor of the people, but, too soon for their interest, they began to raise the price of their lands, which caused many to complain.

A few gentlemen made some attempts to persuade the people to pay no attention to them. I plainly saw that they would work their own ruin, as the greatest security they had for the country would be

(457)

that of making it the interest of the people to support their claim, and that by their conduct they would shortly exasperate the people and that would be the time to overset them. I left the country in the fall of 1775, and returned in the spring following. While in Virginia, I found there were various opinions respecting Henderson & Company's claim. Many thought it was good, others doubted whether or not Virginia could, with propriety, have any pretensions to the country. This was what I wanted to know. I immediately fixed on my plans, viz., that of assembling the people—getting them to elect deputies and sending them to treat with the assembly of Virginia respecting the condition of the country. If valuable conditions were procured, we could declare ourselves citizens of the state; otherwise, we might establish an independent government, and, by giving away a great part of the lands, and disposing of the remainder, we would not only gain great numbers of inhabitants, but in a good measure protect them. To carry this scheme into effect, I appointed a general meeting at Harrodstown, on the 6th of June, 1776, and stated that something would be proposed to the people that very much concerned their interest.

The reason I had for not publishing what I wished to be done before the day was, that the people should not get into parties on the subject, and as everyone would wish to know what was to be done, there would be a more general meeting. But, unfortunately, it was late in the evening of that day before I could get to the place. The people had been in some confusion, but at last concluded that the whole design was to send delegates to the assembly of Virginia with a petition praying the assembly to accept them as such—to establish a new country, etc. The polls were opened, and before I had arrived, they had far advanced in the election, and had entered with such spirit into it that I could not get them to change the principle—that of delegates with petitions, to that of deputies under the authority of the people. In short, I did not take much pains. Mr. John Gabriel Jones and myself were elected. The papers were prepared, and, in a few days, we set out for Williamsburg, in the hope of arriving before the assembly then sitting should rise.

Under great apprehensions that the Indians, under the influence of the British, would shortly make a break upon the country and no time ought to be lost in getting it in a state of defense, and, apprehending no immediate danger in the wilderness road, Mr. Jones and myself attempted to pass, without waiting for other company, but had great cause to regret it. The second day we discovered alarming signs. We were under great apprehensions. On the third day Mr. Jones's horse gave out, and our little put on mine, and in so hilly a country, it was impossible that more than (*one*) could ride at times. The weather being very rainy, our feet being wet for three or four days and nights without ever being dry, not daring to make fire, we both got what hunters call scald feet, a most shocking complaint; the skin seems to rot on every part of our feet; (*in*) this condition we traveled in greater torment than I ever before or since experienced. In hopes of getting relief at the station ten or twelve miles from the Cumberland Gap, in Powell's valley, how greatly were we disappointed on our arrival to find the place totally abandoned and part of it burned. My companion, being but little used to such distress, got almost discouraged at the disappointment. I flattered him in the certainty of the people being at Martin's Fort, about eight miles ahead, as I expected the whole had embodied there, although the danger was much greater than we had apprehended; but being now fully apprised of it, I could, without running very great risk, if we could but make out to march through the woods by both of us riding where there was level ground. This we attempted in vain, and were obliged to take the road, for the person on foot could, by no means, bear the torture of traveling through the thick woods. Hearing guns frequently, we were in hopes they were hunters from the station we were aiming at, but, to our surprise on our arrival, found the fort to have been abandoned for a considerable time.

A few human tracks to be seen, which we knew to be Indians', as well as the guns we had heard, our situation now appeared to be deplorable. The nearest inhabitants we now knew to be sixty miles. Not able to travel ourselves, and Indians appeared to be in full possession of the country that we were in, we sat a few minutes viewing each other. I found myself reduced to a perfect desperation. Mr. Jones asked me what we should do. I told him that it (*was*) impossible for us to make the settlements in the condition that we were in. To hide ourselves in the mountains if the weather was to continue wet, we might probably get worse than better, and perhaps perish; that we knew that within eight or ten days that a party was to follow us from Kentucky; that I knew that oil and ooze made of oak bark would cure our feet in a few days; that I thought that the only plan we could (*adopt*) would be to get possession of the best cabin in the place, fortify ourselves in it, burn down the rest of the fort; abundance of hogs about the corn-cribs—we (*got*) a few of them, a barrel of water and some corn; that we probably (*could*) stand a siege until we were relieved by the party we expected to follow us from Kentucky; that ten or fifteen Indians could not drive us out of the house. I was well acquainted with them, and knew that they would not storm us to a great disadvantage; that we were well armed—a rifle, two cases of good pistols, and a hanger; that I was confident that we could defend ourselves against a greater number of Indians than he had any idea of. He was overjoyed at the proposition, and we fell to work. I sent him to kill a hog by running a sword through it (*when*) it was eating corn, to prevent noise. A small, strong cabin of Captain Martin's, being a little detached from the rest, and locked, having a table and some other things in it, I climbed up to the top of the chimney, and flung it down until it was so low that I could drop into the house without hurting myself, not being able to support myself with my feet against the logs, and cut the lock of the door loose. By this time my friend had got his hog —he being best able to walk—filled a keg with water, and collecting some wood, getting in some corn, we barred (*the*) door, knocked out some port-holes, set the table in the middle of the floor, and spread our arms and ammunition in order, and waited with impatience for

the wind to shift, that we might set fire to the fort without burning
our own castle. Our agreement was, that in case of an attack,
that Mr. Jones should continue to load the pieces as I discharged
them. Without paying any attention to the enemy, except there was
the appearance of a storm, we took some provisions, and meantime dressed our feet with oil and continued to prepare ourselves for
defense with diligence until late in the evening, when the wind appeared to die away, we proposed setting fire to the houses, as we intended, but we had no sooner unbarred our door than we heard a
horse-bell upon the road, and in a few minutes stop again. We were
finally convinced that the enemy was at hand, and immediately secured ourselves as well as possible, determined to execute our first
plan, and if they should attempt to burn us out, to knock off the roof
of the cabin. We waited in suspense for some time, but at last, to
our great joy, found they were white men who had come from
the settlement of Clinch river to collect some things they had hid at
the time they had left the place. The bell of one of their horses happened unstopped when they got within sight of the fort, when they
discovered the smoke of our fire; supposing us to be Indians, they
crept round in order to make a full discovery and get the advantage
of us. While at this business we had a full view of them, and
showed ourselves to them. They appeared to be happy in having it
in their power to relieve us. With them we crossed the mountains
to the settlement, recruiting ourselves.

We proceeded on our journey as far as Botetourt county, and there
learned that we were too late, for the assembly had already risen.

We were now at a loss for some time to determine what to do, but
concluded that we should wait until the fall session; in the meantime,
I should go to Williamsburg and attempt to procure some powder for
the Kentuckians and watch their interests. We parted. Mr. Jones
returned to Holston to join the forces that were raising, in order to
repel the Cherokee Indians (as they had lately commenced hostilities),
and myself proceeded to the governor of Virginia.

Mr. Henry, the governor, lay sick at his seat in Hanover, where I waited on him and produced my vouchers. He appeared much disposed to favor the Kentuckians, and wrote, by me, to the council on the subject. I attended them. My application was for five hundred pounds of powder only, to be conveyed to Kentucky as an immediate supply. After various questions and consultations, the council agreed to furnish the supply; but, as we were a detached people and not yet united to the state of Virginia, and uncertain until the sitting of the assembly whether we should be or not, they would only lend us the ammunition as friends in distress, but that I must become answerable for it in case the assembly should not receive us as citizens of the state. I informed them that it was out of my power to pay the expense of carriage and guards necessary for those supplies; that the British officers on our frontiers were making use of every effort to engage the Indians in the war; that the people might be destroyed for the want of this small supply, and that I was in hopes they would consider these matters and favor us by sending the ammunition at public expense. They replied that they were really disposed to do everything for us in their power consistent with their office, which I believed. After making use of many arguments to convince me that even what they proposed was a stretch of power, they informed me that ' 'they could venture no further." An order was issued to the keeper of the magazine to deliver me the ammunition. I had for twelve months past reflected so much on the various situation of things respecting ourselves and the continent at large, that my resolution was formed before I left the council chamber. I resolved to return the order I had received and immediately repair to Kentucky, knowing that the people would readily fall into my first plan—as what had passed had almost reduced it to a certainty of success. I wrote to the council and inclosed the order, informing them that I had weighed the matter and found that it was out of my power to convey those stores at my own expense such a distance through an enemy's country; that I was sorry to find we should have to seek protection elsewhere, which I did not doubt of getting; that if a country was not worth protecting it was not worth claiming, etc. What passed on the reception of this letter I can not tell. It was, I suppose, nothing more than what might be expected by a set of gentlemen zealous in welfare of their country and fully apprised of what they might expect to take place in Kentucky. I was sent for. Being a little prejudiced in favor of my mother country, I was willing to meet half way. Orders were immediately issued, dated August 23d, 1776, for conveying those stores to Pittsburg and there to await further orders from me.

Things being amicably settled, I wrote to Kentucky giving information of what I had done, and recommended them to send to Pittsburg and convey the ammunition by water to their own country. This they never received. I waited until the fall session, when I was joined by my colleague, Mr. Jones. We laid our papers before the assembly. They resolved that we could not take our seats as members, but that our business should be attended to. Colonel Henderson, one of the purchasers of the Cherokees, being present, retarded our business much. Colonel Arthur Campbell, one of the members, being also opposed to our having a new county, wished us annexed to the county on the frontiers of which we lay and which he represented. This caused it to be late in the session (December 7, 1776) before we got a complete establishment of a new county by the name of Kentucky.

Mr. Jones and myself parted at Williamsburg, but, learning that the ammunition was yet at Pittsburg, we resolved to go by that post and take it down the river. We agreed to meet there, but the weather proving severe, it was late in the fall before we could set out, but, however trifling a small quantity of ammunition or the loss or acquisition of a few men may appear in the scale of affairs among people in general, to the Kentuckians the loss of either I knew would be sensibly felt, of course paid every attention possible. I found that the Indians were fully preparing for war in the spring; that those of them who attended Fort Pitt, under the color of friendship, were in fact acting as spies; that they had some idea of our intentions of going down the river, and would attempt to intercept us. Sensible that our safety depended solely on expedition, without waiting to recruit our party, we set out with seven hands only in a small vessel, and, by the most indefatigable labor, made our way good. We passed the Indians in the night, or by some means or other got ahead of them, for the day before we landed near Limestone, we plainly discovered that they were in pursuit of us. We hid our stores in four or five different places and considerable distance apart, and running a few miles lower in our vessel, set it adrift and took by land for Harrodstown in order to get force sufficient and return ourselves for our stores. We parted by the Blue Lick, and the third day from our leaving the river got to Hinkston's cabin, on the west side of Licking creek. While we were resting ourselves, four men came to us who had been exploring land in that quarter, and informed us of the situation of affairs in Kentucky; that very little damage had yet been done; that the late Colonel John Todd was with a party somewhere in that part of country; that, if we could find him, we should be strong enongh to return to the river, but this was uncertain. As several of our party were much fatigued we agreed that myself and two others should proceed to Harrodstown for the proposed party; that Mr. Jones and the rest should remain in that neighborhood until our return.

In a short time after I had set our, Colonel Todd arrived at the same place, and, after some consultation, concluded that they were able to go to the river and bring on the ammunition and other stores, and accordingly set out with ten men, and between the Blue Lick and the river, on December 25, met the Indians on our trail and got totally routed. Mr. Jones was killed, and three others got killed and taken prisoners. Fortunately for us, the prisoners did not discover our hidden stores to the Indians. The party sent from Harrodstown brought them safe to that place, which gave universal joy.

On the 29th December, a large party of Indians attacked McClellan's fort, on Elkhorn, and killed Mr. McClellan and White and wounded two others, after which the whole moved to Harrodstown. The inhabitants of Kentucky, at this period, consisted only of about—

men in three stations, Harrodstown, Boonesborough, and Colonel Logan's about this time established. The information I gave sufficiently alarmed them. The people had scarcely time to prepare themselves before a large body of Indians advanced on the 7th of March (on the 5th the militia of the country was embodied), to the attack of Harrodstown. They fired on some boys in the evening five miles from town; held one, the rest made .their escape and gave the alarm. A party from the fort advanced to the place. It being late in the evening, they, fortunately, did not fall in with the Indians, as in all probability our party could have been cut to pieces and of course the country lost. The loss of a single man at this time was sensibly felt, and general actions with the enemy ought to be guarded against without an apparent superiority, as the enemy could easily retrieve their losses by recruits from numerous nations, which was an advantage we could not expect to enjoy for some time. In the morning following, the Indians had waylaid the upper part of the town (that had been evacuated the evening before), and a little after daylight set fire to one of the houses. A small party unadvisedly went to see what was the cause and was fired on by the Indians; they were covered by a party from the fort and made good their retreat. In this affair there was a man lost, killed, on each side, and a few wounded. Being the superior officer, we had the country put in as good a state of defense as our situation would admit of, determined, if possible, to stand our ground in hopes of relief, as the governor of Virginia had uniformly appeared to be our friend.

From this period we may date the commencement of that bloody war in Kentucky that has continued since with savage fury, in which, on a moderate calculation, upwards of two thousand souls have perished on our soil, and severely felt by the most active Indian nations. To enumerate all the little actions that happened, is impossible. They were continual and severe, when compared to our small forces; tne forts were often attacked; policy seemed to have required that the whole should be embodied in one place, but depending on hunting for the greater part of our provisions forbid it. No people could be

30

in a more alarming situation. Detached at least two hundred miles from the nearest settlements of the states, surrounded by numerous nations of Indians, each one far superior to ourselves in numbers and under the influence of the British government and pointedly directed to destroy us, as appeared by instruments of writing left on the back of people killed by them—I was frequently afraid the people would think of making their peace with Detroit and suffer themselves and families to be carried off. Their distress may be easily conceived from our situation, but they yet remained firm in hopes of relief, which they received by the arrival of a company of men under the command of Colonel John Bowman, on the 2d of September.

This reinforcement, though small, added new life to the appearance of things. Encouraged by this, and the stand they had already made, everyone seemed determined to exert himself in strengthening the country by encouraging as many of his friends as possible to move out, which succeeded in the end. After the arrival of Colonel Bowman I left Kentucky, in October, 1777, with a party of young men, who had been detained on the promise of being liberated on the arrival of Colonel Bowman, and returned to Virginia. During the past severe spring and summer our conduct was very uniform. The defense of our forts, the procuring of provisions, and, when possible, suppressing the Indians (which was frequently done), burying the dead and dressing the wounded, seemed to be all our business.

The whole of my time when not employed in reflecting on things in general, particularly Kentucky, how it accorded with the interest of the United States, whether it was to their interest to support her, etc. This led me to a long train of thinking, the result of which was to lay aside every private view, engage seriously in the war and have the interest and welfare of the public my only view until the fate of the fall of the continent should be known. Divesting myself of the prejudice and partiality in favor of any particular part of the community, but so pursue what I conceived to be the interest of the whole. This path influenced my conduct through the course of the war and enabled me to better judge of the importance of Kentucky to the Union, situated, as it was, in the center, almost, of the Indians, who had already generally engaged in the Kentucky war, as an impediment in their way to the more interior frontier; that as soon as they should accomplish the destruction of it they would bodily let loose on the frontier; that, instead of the states receiving supplies from them, they would be obliged to keep large bodies of troops for their defense, and almost impossible to move an enemy at so great a distance to attack their towns, if they could find them; and that, by supporting and encouraging the growth of Kentucky, those obstacles would, in a great measure, be removed; for, should the British officers find their policy mistaken in carrying on the war against Kentucky by the Indians, and withdraw them from and bind their whole force against the interior frontier, as a certain mode of destroying the states, we might, with a little assistance, at any time, march from the country with ease to any part of their country we chose (this is the only circumstance that can excuse their conduct). Those ideas caused me to view Kentucky in the most favorable point of view, as a place of the greatest consequence, and ought to meet with every encouragement, and that nothing that I could engage in would be of more general utility than its defense, and as the commandants of the different towns of the Illinois and Wabash, I knew, were busily engaged in exciting the Indians, their reduction became my first object. Expecting, probably, that it might open a field for further action, I sent two young hunters (S. More and B. Linn) to those places as spies, with proper instructions for their conduct, to prevent suspicion. Neither did they, nor anyone in Kentucky, ever know my design until it was ripe for execution. They returned to Harrodstown with all the information I could reasonably have expected. I found from them that they had but little expectation of a visit from us, but that things were kept in good order, the militia trained, etc., that they might, in case of a visit, be prepared; that the greatest pains were taken to inflame the minds of the French inhabitants against the Americans, notwithstanding they could discover traces of affection in some of the inhabitants; that the Indians in that quarter were engaged in the war, etc.

When I left Kentucky, October 1st, 1777, I plainly saw that every eye was turned toward me, as if expecting some stroke in their favor. Some doubted my return, expecting I would join the army in Virginia. I left them with reluctance, promising that I would certainly return to their assistance, which I had predetermined. On my arrival at Williamsburg I remained a considerable time, settling the accounts of the Kentucky militia and (*noting*) remarks of everything I saw or heard that could lead me to the knowledge of the disposition of those in power. Burgoyne's army having been captured, and things seeming to wear a pleasing aspect, on the 10th December I communicated my views to Governor Henry. At first he seemed to be fond of it; but to detach a party at so great a distance (although the service performed might be of great utility) appeared daring and hazardous, as nothing but secrecy could give success to the enterprise. To lay the matter before the assembly, then sitting, would be dangerous, as it would soon be known throughout the frontiers; and probably the first prisoner taken by the Indians would give the alarm, which would end in the certain destruction of the party. He had several private councils, composed of select gentlemen. After making every inquiry into my proposed plans of operation (and particularly that of a retreat, in case of misfortune, across the Mississippi into the Spanish territory), the expedition was resolved upon; and as an encouragement to those who would engage in said service, an instrument of writing was signed, wherein those gentlemen promised to use their influence to procure from the assembly three hundred acres of land for each in case of success. The governor and council so warmly engaged in the success of this enterprise that I had very little trouble in getting matters adjusted; and on the second day of January, 1778, received my instructions and £1,200 for the use of the expedition, with an order on Pittsburg for boats, ammunition, etc. Finding, from the governor's conversation in general to me on the subject, that he did not wish an implicit attention to his instructions should prevent my executing anything that would manifestly tend to the good of the public, on the 4th I set forward, clothed with all the authority that I wished. I advanced to Major William B. Smith £150, to recruit men on Holston, and to meet me in Kentucky. (He never joined me.) Captain Leonard Helm, of Fauquier, and Captain Joseph Bowman, of Frederick, were to raise each a company, and on the 1st of February I arrived at Red Stone.*

Being now in the country where all arrangements were to be made, I appointed Captain William Harrod and many other officers to the recruiting service, and contracted for flour and other stores that I wanted. General Hand then commanded at Pitt, and promised a supply of the articles I had orders for. I received information from Captain Helm that several gentlemen in that quarter took pains to counteract his interest in recruiting, as no such service was known of by the assembly. Consequently, he had to send to the governor to get his conduct ratified. I found, also, opposition to our interest in the Pittsburg country. As the whole was divided into violent parties between the Virginians and Pennsylvanians respecting territory, each trying to counteract the idea of men being raised for the state of Virginia affected the vulgar of one party; and, as my real instructions were kept concealed, and only an instrument from the governor, written designedly for deception, was made public, wherein I was authorized to raise men for the defense of Kentucky, many gentlemen of both parties conceived it to be injurious to the public interest to draw off men at so critical a moment for the defense of a few detached inhabitants, who had better be removed, etc. These circumstances caused some confusion in the recruiting service. On the 29th March I received a letter from Major Smith by express, informing me that he had raised four companies on the Holston, to be marched immediately to Kentucky, agreeably to his orders; and an express from Kentucky informed me that they had much strengthened since I left that quarter. This information of four companies being raised, with Bowman's and Helm's, which I knew were on their way to join me

*Now Brownsville, Pennsylvania, on the river Monongahela.

at Red Stone, caused me to be more easy respecting recruits than otherwise I should have been. The officers only got such as had friends in Kentucky, or those induced by their own interest and desire to see the country. Meeting with several disappointments, it was late in May before I could leave the Red Stone settlement with those companies and a considerable number of families and private adventurers. Taking in my stores at Pittsburg and Wheeling, I proceeded down the river with caution.

On our arrival at the mouth of the Great Kanawha, Captain Arbuckle, the commandant, informed us that about 250 Indians had warmly attacked his post the day before and wounded a few of his men; that the enemy had directed their course to the settlements of Greenbrier; that he had sent out (an) express to give the alarm; that, if I thought it prudent, he was sensible that the forces I had, with the addition of part of the garrison, could, in all probability, overtake them before they got to the settlement and give them a total rout. The prospect was flattering, but uncertainty of getting the advantage of the enemy, the loss of the time and perhaps a number of men, which (would) end in the destruction of the enterprise that I was on, and the almost certainty of the frontiers getting the alarm by the express in time might repel them, which they did. Those ideas induced me to decline it. I proceeded on, being joined by Captain James O'Hara on his way to the Arkansas on public business. I landed at the mouth of Kentucky, where I intended to have fortified, as the growth of Kentucky greatly depended on a post being fixed on the Ohio river, and a place of security for the emigrants that wished to come down the river; but, taking in view my designs to be westward, I found that Kentucky was not the spot except we could afford to keep two posts. In case of success, it would be absolutely necessary to have a post of communication on the river between the Illinois and Kentucky, and of course the falls was the most eligible spot as it would answer all the more desirable purposes, and in a great measure protect the navigation of the river, as every vessel would be obliged to stop some time at that place. They would be always exposed to the Indians.

I had learned that but one company, Captain Dillard's, of Major Smith's troops, had yet arrived in Kentucky, which alarmed me, as I was afraid the disappointment would prove fatal to our schemes. I wrote to Colonel Bowman, informed him of my intention of fixing a garrison at the falls, and that I had an object in view of the greatest importance to the country; desired him to meet me there with what troops there was of Major Smith's, and what militia could be spared with safety from the different posts.

I moved on to the falls and viewed the different situations, but, reflecting that my secret instructions were yet unknown, even to the party with me, and not knowing what would be the consequences when they should be divulged on our being joined by the whole, I wished to have everything (*secure*) as much as possible. I observed the little island of about (*seventy* ?) acres, opposite to where the town of Louisville now stands, seldom or never was entirely covered by the water. I resolved to take possession and fortify (*it*), which I did on —th of June, dividing the island among the families for gardens. These families that followed me I now found to be of real service, as they were of little expense, and, with the invalids, would keep possession of this little post until we should be able to occupy the main shore, which happened in the fall, agreeable to instructions I had sent from the Illinois. The people on the Monongahela, learning by (*word*) I had sent them of this post, great numbers had moved down. This was one of the principal, among other, causes of the rapid progress of the settlement of Kentucky.

On the arrival of Colonel (*John*) Bowman, part of the militia and several of the gentlemen of the country, we found, on examination, that we were much weaker than expected, and the Indians continued, without intermission, and were more numerous the longer they continued, as the British continued to add to their strength by exciting others to join them. Under those circumstances we could not think of leaving the posts of Kentucky defenseless; that it was better to

run a great risk with one party than to divide our forces in such manner as to hazard the loss of both; of course, we agreed to take but
one complete company and part of another from Kentucky, expecting
that they would be replaced by troops we yet expected from Major
Smith. Those were our deliberations. After my making known my
instructions almost every gentleman warmly espoused the enterprise,
and plainly saw the utility of it, and supposed they saw the salvation
of Kentucky almost in their reach; but some repined that we were
not strong enough to put it beyond all doubt. The soldiery, in general, debated on the subject, but determined to follow their officers;
some were alarmed at the thought of being taken at so great a distance into the enemy's country, that if they should have success in the
first instance they might be attacked in their posts without a possibility of getting succor or making their retreat. Spies were continually
among the whole. Some dissatisfaction was discovered in Captain
Dillard's company, consequently, the boats were well secured and
sentinels placed where it (*was*) thought there was a possibility of
their wading from the island. My design was to take those from the
island down on our way who would not attempt to desert, but got out-
generaled by their lieutenant, whom I had previously conceived a
very tolerable opinion of. They had, by swimming in the day, discovered that the channel opposite their camp might be waded, and a
little before day himself and the greater part of the company slipped
down the bank and got to the opposite shore before they were discovered
by the sentinels. Vexed at the idea of their escape in the manner
they did, as one of my principal motives for taking post on the island
was to prevent desertion, and, intending to set out the next day, I was
undetermined for (*a*) few minutes what to do, as it might take a party
several days to overtake (*them*), and, having no distrust of those who
remained, the example was not immediately dangerous but might prove
so hereafter; and recollecting that there was a number of horses
(*belonging*) to gentlemen from Harrodsburg, I ordered a strong party
to pursue them, and for the foot and horse to relieve each other regularly, and so put to death every man in their power who would

not surrender. They overhauled them in about twenty miles. The deserters, discovering them at a distance, scattered in the woods; only seven or eight were taken. The rest made their way to the different posts; many who were not woodsmen almost perished. The poor lieutenant, and few who remained with him, after suffering almost all that could be felt from hunger and fatigue, arrived at Harrodstown. Having heard of his conduct (*they*) would not, for some time, suffer him to come into their houses, nor give him anything to eat.

On the return of the party, the soldiers hung and burnt his effigy. Every preparation was made for our departure. After spending a day of amusement in parting with our friends of Kentucky, they to return to the defense of their country and we in search of new adventures.

On the (*24th*) of June, 1778, we left our little island and run about a mile up the river in order to gain the main channel, and shot the falls at the very moment of the sun being in a great eclipse, which caused various conjectures among the superstitious. As I knew that spies were kept on the river, below the towns of the Illinois, I had resolved to march part of the way by land, and, of course, left the whole of our baggage, except as much as would equip us in the Indian mode. The whole of our force, after leaving such as were judged not competent to the expected fatigue, consisted only of four companies, commanded by Captains John Montgomery, Joseph Bowman, Leonard Helm and William Harrod. My force being so small to what I expected, owing to the various circumstances already mentioned, I found it necessary to alter my plans of operations.

As post St. Vincennes at this time was a town of considerable force, consisting of near four hundred militia, with an Indian town adjoining, and great numbers continually in the neighborhood, and in the scale of Indian affairs of more importance than any other, I had thought of attacking it first, but now found that I could by no means venture near it. I resolved to begin my career in the Illinois where there were more inhabitants, but scattered in different villages, and less danger of being immediately overpowered by the Indians; in case of necessity, we could probably make our retreat to the Spanish side of the Mississippi, but if successful, we might pave our way to the possession of Post St. Vincent.

I had fully acquainted myself that the French inhabitants in those western settlements had great influence among the Indians in general, and were more beloved by them (*the Indians*) than any other Europeans—that their commercial intercourse was universal throughout the western and northwestern countries—and that the governing interest on the lakes was mostly in the hands of the English, who were not much beloved by them.

These, and many other ideas similar thereto, caused me to resolve, if possible, to strengthen myself by such train of conduct as might probably attach the (*French inhabitants*) to our interest and give us influence at a greater distance than the (*limits of the*) country we were aiming for. These were the principles that influenced my future conduct; and, fortunately, I had just received a letter from Colonel Campbell, dated Pittsburg, informing me of the contents of the treaties between France and America.

As I intended to leave the Ohio at Fort Massac, three leagues below the Tennessee, I landed on a small island (Barrataria ?) in the mouth of that river, in order to prepare for the march. In a few hours after, one John Duff and a party of hunters coming down the river were brought to by our boats. They were men formerly from the states, and assured us of their happiness in the adventure (their surprise having been owing to their not knowing who we were). They had been but lately from Kaskaskia, and were able to give us all the intelligence we wished. They said that Governor Abbott had lately left Post Vincennes and gone to Detroit on some business of importance; that Mr. Rochblave commanded Kaskaskia; that the militia was kept in good order, and spies on the Mississippi; and that all hunters, both Indians and others, were ordered to keep a good lookout for the rebels; that the fort was kept in good order as an asylum, etc.; but they believed the whole to proceed more from the fondness for parade than the expectation of a visit; that they were convinced that if they received timely notice of us they would collect and give us a warm reception, as they were taught to harbor a most horrid idea of the barbarity of rebels, especially the Virginians; but that, if we could surprise the place, which they were in hopes we might, they made no doubt of our being able to do as we pleased; that they hoped to be received as partakers in the enterprise, and wished us to put full confidence in them, and they would assist the guides in conducting the party. This was agreed to, and they proved valuable men.

The acquisition to us was great, as I had no intelligence from these posts since the spies I sent twelve months past. But no part of their information pleased me more than that of the inhabitants viewing us as more savage than their neighbors, the Indians. I was determined to improve upon this if I was fortunate enough to get them into my possession, and conceived the greater the shock I could give them at first the more sensibly would they feel my lenity, and become more valuable friends. This I conceived to be agreeable to human nature, as I had observed it in many instances. Having everything prepared, we moved down to a little gully, a small distance above Massac, in which we concealed our boats, and set out a northwestern course. Nothing remarkable on this route. The weather was favorable; in some parts water was scarce as well as game; of course we suffered drought and hunger, but not to excess. On the third day, John Saunders, our principal guide, appeared confused, and we soon discovered that he was totally lost, without there was some other cause of his present conduct. I asked him various questions, and from his answers could scarcely determine what to think of him, whether or not ne was sensible that he was lost or that he wished to deceive us. The cry of the whole detachment was that he was a traitor. He begged that he might be suffered to go some distance into a plain that was in full view, to try to make some discovery whether or not he was right. I told him he might go, but that I was suspicious of him from his conduct; that from the first day of his being employed he always said he knew the way well; that there was now a different appearance; that I saw the nature of the country was such that a person once acquainted with it could not, in a short time, forget it; that a few men should go with him to prevent his escape, and that if he did not discover and take us into the hunter's road that led from the east into Kaskaskia, that he had frequently described, I would have him immediately put to death, which I was determined to have done; but after a search of an hour or two he came to a place that he knew perfectly, and we discovered that the poor fellow had been, as they call it, bewildered.

On the 4th of July, in the evening, we got within a few miles of the town, where we lay until near dark, keeping spies ahead, after which we commenced our march and took possession of a house wherein a large family lived, on the bank of the Kaskaskia river about three-quarters of a mile above the town, where we were informed that the people, a few days before, were under arms, but had concluded that the cause of the alarm was without foundation, and that at that time there was a great number of men in town, but that the Indians had generally left it, and at present all was quiet. We soon procured a sufficiency of vessels, the more in ease to convey us across the river, (and) formed the party into three divisions. I was now convinced that it was impossible that the inhabitants could make any resistance, as they could not now possibly get notice of us time enough to make much resistance. My object now was to conduct matters so as to get possession of the place with as little confusion as possible, but to have it even at the loss of the whole town. Not perfectly relying on the information we got at the house, as he seemed to vary in his information, and as (a noise) was just heard in town, which he informed us he supposed was the negroes at a dance, etc.

With one of the divisions, I marched to the fort and ordered the other two into different quarters of the town. If I met with no resistance, at a certain signal, a general shout was to be given, and certain parts were to be immediately possessed, and the men of each detachment who could speak the French language were to run through every street and proclaim what had happened, and inform the inhabitants that every person who appeared in the streets would be shot down. This disposition had its desired effect. In a very little time we had complete possession, and every avenue was guarded to prevent any escape to give the alarm to the other villages, in case of opposition. Various orders had been issued not worth mentioning. I don't suppose greater silence ever reigned among the inhabitants of a place than did at present; not a person to be seen, not a word to be heard from them for some time; but, designedly, the greatest noise kept up by our troops through every quarter of the town, and patrols continually the whole night round it, as intercepting any information was a capital object, and in about two hours the whole of the inhabitants were disarmed, and informed that if one was taken attempting to make his escape, he would be immediately put to death.

Mr. Rochblave was secured, but, as it had been some time before he could be got out of his room, I suppose it was in order to inform his lady what to do—I suppose to secure his public letters, etc., as but few were got; his chambers not being visited for the night, she had full opportunity of doing (*so*), but by what means we never could learn—I don't suppose among her trunks, although they never were examined. She must have expected the loss of even her clothes, from the idea she entertained of us. Several particular persons were sent for, in the course of the night, for information, etc., but (*we*) got very little (*beyond*) what we already knew, except, from the conduct of several persons then in town, there was reason to suppose they were inclined to the American interest; that a great number of Indians had been, and was then, in the neighborhood of Kaskaskia (Kahokia ?), sixty miles from this; that a Mr. Cerre, a principal merchant, one of the most inveterate enemies we had, left the place a few days past, with a large quantity of furs for Michilimackinac, from thence to Quebec, from (*whence*) he had lately arrived; that he was then in St. Louis, the Spanish capital; that his lady and family were then (*in*) town, with a very considerable quantity of goods, etc. I imme-

diately suspected what those informers aimed at—that of making
their peace with me at the expense of their neighbors.   My situation
required too much caution to give them much satisfaction.   I found
that Mr. Cerre was one of the most eminent men in the country, of
great influence among the people.   I had some suspicion that his
accusers were probably in debt to him and wished to ruin him; but,
from observations I had made, from what I had heard of him, he became an object of consequence to me; that perhaps he might be
wavering in his opinion respecting the contest; that, if he should take
a decisive part in our favor, he might be a valuable acquisition.   In
short, his enemies caused me much to wish to see (*him*), and, as he
was then out of my power, I made no doubt of bringing it about,
through the means of his family, having them then in my power.   I
had a guard immediately placed at his house, his stores sealed, etc.,
as well as all others, making no doubt but that when he heard of this
he would be extremely anxious to get an interview.   Messrs. R.
Winston and Daniel Murray, who proved to have been in the American interest, by the morning of the 5th, had plenty of provisions
prepared.   After the troops had regaled themselves, they were withdrawn from within the town, and I posted (*them*) in different positions on the border of it, and I had every person expressly forbid
holding any conversation with the inhabitants.   All was distrust;
their town in complete possession of an enemy whom they entertained the most horrid idea of, and not yet being able to have any
conversation with one of our people, even those that I had conversation with were ordered not to speak to the rest.   After some time
they were informed that they (*could*) walk freely about the town.
After finding they were busy in conversation, I had a few of the
principal militia officers put in irons, without naming a reason for it
or hearing anything they had to say in their own defense.   The worst
was now expected by the whole.   I saw the consternation the inhabitants were in, and I suppose, in imagination, felt all they experienced in reality, and felt myself disposed to act as an arbiter between
them and my duty.

After some time, the priest got permission to wait on me. He came with five or six elderly gentlemen with him. However shocked they already were, from their present situation, the addition was obvious and great when they entered the room where I was sitting with the other officers, (*all in*) a dirty, savage appearance, as we had left our clothes at the river (*and*) we were almost naked, and torn by the bushes and briers. They were shocked, and it was some time before they would venture to take seats, and longer before they would speak. They at last were asked what they wanted. The priest informed me (after asking which was the principal), that, as the inhabitants expected to be separated, never, perhaps, to meet again, they begged, through him, that they might be permitted to spend some time in the church, to take their leave of each other. I knew they expected their very religion was obnoxious to us. I carelessly told him I had nothing to say to his church; that he might go there if he would; if he did, to inform the people not to venture out of the town. They attempted some other conversation, but were informed that we were not at leisure. They went off, after answering me a few questions that I asked them, with a very faint degree (*of hope*) that they might (*not be*) totally discouraged from coming again, as they had not yet come to the point I wanted. The whole town seemed to have collected to the church; infants were carried, and the houses generally left without a person in them, (*except*) it was such as cared but little how things went, and a few others who were not so much alarmed. Orders were given to prevent the soldiers from entering a house. They remained a considerable time in church, after which the priest and many of the principal men came to me to return thanks for the indulgence shown them, and begged permission to address me farther on the subject that was more dear to them than anything else; that their present situation was the fate of war; that the loss of their property they could reconcile, but were in hopes that I would not part them from their families; and that the women and children might be allowed to keep some of their clothes and a small quantity of provisions. They were in hopes by industry, that they might support them; that their whole conduct had been influenced by their commanders, whom they looked upon themselves bound to obey; and that they were not certain of being acquainted with the nature of the American war, as they had had but little opportunity to inform themselves; that many of them frequently expressed themselves as much in favor of the Americans as they dare to. In short, they said everything that could be supposed that sensible men in their alarming situation would advance.

All they appeared to aim at was some lenity shown their women and families, supposing that their goods would appease us. I had sufficient reason to believe that there was no finesse in this, but that they really spoke their sentiments and the heights of their expectation. This was the point I wanted to bring them to. I asked them very abruptly whether or not they thought they were speaking to savages; that I was certain they did from the tenor of their conversation. Did they suppose that we meant to strip the women and children, or take the bread out of their mouths, or that we would condescend to make war on the women and children or the church? It was to prevent the effusion of innocent blood by the Indians, through the instigation of their commanders' emissaries, that caused us to visit them, and not the prospect of plunder; that as soon as that object was attained, we should be perfectly satisfied; that as the king of France had joined the Americans, there was a probability of there shortly being an end to the war (this information very apparently affected them). They were at liberty to take which side they pleased, without any dread of losing their property or having their families destroyed. As for their church, all religions would be tolerated in America, and so far from our intermeddling with it, that any insult offered to it should be punished; and to convince them that we were not savages and plunderers, as they had conceived, that they might return to their families and inform them that they might conduct themselves as usual, with all freedom and without apprehensions of any danger; that from the information I had got since my arrival, so fully convinced me of their being influenced by false information from their leaders, that I was willing to forget everything past; that their friends in confinement should immediately be released, and the guard withdrawn from every part of the town, except Cerre's, and that I only required compliance to a proclamation. This was the substance of my reply to them. They wished to soften the idea of my conceiving that they supposed us to be savages and plunderers; that they had conceived that the property in all towns belonged to those that reduced it, etc. I informed them that I knew that they were taught to believe that we were but little better than barbarians, but that we would say no more on the subject; that I wished them to go and relieve the anxiety of the inhabitants. Their feelings must be more easily guessed than expressed. They retired, and, in a few minutes, the scene was changed from an almost mortal dejection, to that of joy in the extreme—the bells ringing, the church crowaed, returning thanks, in short, every appearance of extravagant joy that could fill a place with almost confusion. I immediately set about preparing a proclamation to be presented to them before they left the church; but wishing to prove the people further, I omitted it for a few days, as I made no doubt but that any report that would be now made of us through the country would be favorable.

I was more careless who went or came into the town; but, not knowing what might happen, I yet (*felt*) uneasy as (*to*) Kohokia, and was determined to make a lodgment there as soon as possible, and gain the place by something similar to what had been done. I ordered Major Bowman to mount his company and part of another, and a few inhabitants, to inform their friends what had happened, on horses procured from the town, and proceed without delay, and if possible get possession of Kohokia before the ensuing morning; that I should give him no further instructions on the subject, but for him to make use of his own prudence. He gave orders for collecting the horses, on which numbers of the gentlemen came, and informed me that they were sensible of the design; that the troops were much fatigued; that they (*thought*) I would not take it amiss at their offering themselves to execute whatever I should wish to be done at Kohokia;

3 I

that the people were their friends and relations, and would follow
their example—at least they hoped that they might be permitted to
accompany the detachment. Conceiving that it might be good policy to
show them that we felt confidence in them—and this (*was*) in fact what
I wished for from obvious reasons—I informed them that I made no
doubt but that Major Bowman would be fond of their company, and
that as many as chose it might go, though we were too weak to be
otherways than suspicious, and much on our guard; and knowing
that we had a sufficient security for their good behavior, I told them
(*if*) they went they ought to equip for war, although I was in hopes
that every(*thing*) would be amicably settled; but, as it was the first
time they ever bore arms as free men, it might be well to equip themselves and try how they felt as such, especially as they were going to
put their friends in the same situation, etc. (*They*) appeared highly
pleased at the idea, and in the evening the major set out with a troop
but a little inferior to the one we had marched into the country. The
French being commanded by the famous militia officers, those new
friends of ours were so elated at thought of the parade they were to
make at Kohokia, that they were too much engaged in equipping themselves to appear to the best advantage, that it was night before the
party moved, and the distance twenty leagues, that it was late in the
morning of the 6th before they reached Kohokia. Detaining every
person they met with, they got into the border of the town before
they were discovered. The inhabitants were at first much alarmed
at being thus suddenly visited by strangers in a hostile appearance,
and ordered to surrender the town, even by their friends and relations; but as the confusion among the women and children appeared
greater than they expected, from the cry of the big knife being in
town, they immediately assembled and gave the people a detail of
what had happened at Kaskaskia. The major informed them not to
be alarmed; that though resistance at present was out of the question, he would convince them that he would prefer their friendship
than otherwise; that he was authorized to inform them that they
were at liberty to become free Americans, as their friends at Kaskas-

kia had, or (*they*) that did not choose it might (*go*) out of the country, except those who had been engaged in inciting the Indians to war.

Liberty and freedom, and huzzaing for the Americans, rang through the whole town. The Kaskaskian gentlemen disappeared among their friends. In a few hours the whole was amicable, and Major Bowman snugly quartered in the old British fort. Some individuals said that the town was given up too tamely, but little attention was paid to them. A considerable number of Indians was encamped in the neighborhood, as this was a principal post of trade, immediately fled; one of them, who was at St. Louis some time after this, got a letter written to me excusing himself for not paying me a visit. By the 8th Major Bowman got everything settled agreeable to our wishes. The whole of the inhabitants took the oath of allegiance cheerfully. He set about repairing the fort and regulating the internal police of the place, etc. The intermediate villages followed the example of the others, and, as a strict examination was not made as to those who had a hand in encouraging the Indians to war, in a few days the country appeared to be in a most perfect state of harmony. A friendly correspondence immediately sprung up between the Spanish officers and ourselves, (*and*) added much to the general tranquillity and happiness, but, as to myself, enjoyments of this nature were not my fortune. I found myself launched into a field that would require great attention, and all the address I was master of, to extricate myself from in doing that service to my country which appeared now in full view, with honor to them and credit to myself, as I could now get every piece of information I wished for. I was astonished at the pains and expense the British were at in engaging the Indians, and that they had emissaries in every nation throughout those extensive countries, and even bringing the inhabitants of Lake Superior by water to Detroit and fitting them out from thence; that the sound of war was universal among them; scarcely a nation but what had declared it and received the bloody belt and hatchet. Post St. Vincent I found to be a place of infinite importance to us. To gain it was now my object, but, sensible that all the forces we had, joined by every man in Kentucky, would not be able to approach it, I resolved on other measures than that of arms. I determined to send no message to the Indians for some time, but, wishing for interviews between us to happen, through the means of the French gentlemen, and appear careless myself, and all the titles I gave myself unnecessaries, etc. The falls of Ohio was mentioned (*in order to have them believe*) that the troops we had were only a detachment from that place, though sufficient to answer our purpose; that the body of our force was there fortifying; that great numbers more were daily expected to arrive, from whence we intended to proceed to war; every man we had was taught to speak in this strain. From many hints and (*from*) information of mine before I left that place, the greatest part of them believed the most of this to be true. In short, anxious for our marching into the Illinois with so small a force, was really necessary. This idea had, at an early period, struck me. I inquired particularly into the manner the people had been governed formerly, and much to my satisfaction, (*I found*) that it had been generally as severe as under the militia law. I was determined to make an advantage of it, and took every step in my power to cause the people to feel the blessings enjoyed by an American citizen, which I soon discovered enabled me to support, from their own choice, almost a supreme authority over them. I caused a court of civil judication to be established at Kohokia, elected by the people. Major Bowman, to the surprise of the people, held a poll for a magistracy, and was elected and acted as judge of the court. [Manuscript here illegible.] After this similar courts were established in the towns of Kaskaskia and St. Vincent. There was an appeal to myself in certain cases, and I believe that no people ever had their business done more to their satisfaction than they had through the means of these regulations for a considerable time.

Mr. Cerre, formerly mentioned at the time of Major Bowman's arrival at Kohokia, was yet in St. Louis, and, preparing to prosecute his journey to Canada, was stopped in consequence of the information. After learning the situation of things, agreeable to my expectations, he resolved to return; but learning that there was a guard kept at his house, and at no other, and that several had attempted to ruin him by their information to me, (*as*) you were advised, not to venture over without a safe conduct, he applied to the Spanish governor for a letter to that purpose and came to St. Genevieve, opposite to Kaskaskia, and got another from the commandant of that post, to the same purpose, and sent them to me; but all the interest he could make through the channel of the Spanish officers, and the solicitations of his particular friends, which I found to be a great majority of the people, could (*not*) procure him a safe conduct. I absolutely denied it, and hinted that I wished to hear no more on the subject; neither would I hear any person that had anything to say in vindication of him, informing them that I understood that M. Cerre was a sensible man; that if he was innocent of the allegations against him he would not be afraid of delivering himself up; that his backwardness seems to prove his guilt; that I cared very little about him. I suppose a rumor immediately gave him this information. In a few hours he came over, and before visiting his family presented himself before me. I told him that I supposed that he was fully sensible of the charges that were exhibited against (*him*), particularly that of inciting the Indians to murder, etc.—a crime that ought to be punished by all people that should be so fortunate as to get that person in their power; that his late backwardness almost confirmed me in his guilt. He replied that he was a mere merchant; that he never concerned himself about state affairs further than the interest of his trade required; that he had, as yet, no opportunity so fully to acquaint himself with the principle of the present contest as to enable (*him*) finally to settle his own opinion to his satisfaction; that his being generally so far detached from the seat of affairs that he was always doubtful of his only hearing one side of the question; that he had learned more in a few days past than he ever before knew; that it only confirmed his former suspicion. I read him part of a letter from Governor Hamilton of Detroit to Mr. Rochblave, wherein he was alluded to with much affection. He said that when he was there he behaved himself as became a subject; that he defied any man to prove that he ever encouraged an Indian to war; that many had often heard him disapprove the cruelty of such proceedings; that there was a number in town that was much in debt to him—perhaps the object of some of them (*was*) to get clear of it by ruining of him; that it would be inconsistent for him, in his present situation, to offer to declare his present sentiments respecting the war, but wished to stand every test as that of encouraging the Indians is what he ever detested. He excused his fearing coming over the Mississippi as soon as he could have wished. I told him to retire into another room, without making him any further reply. The whole town was anxious to know the fate of Mr. Cerre. I sent for his accusers—a great number following them—and had Mr. Cerre called. I plainly saw the confusion his appearance made among them. I opened the case to the whole—told them that I never chose to condemn a man unheard; that Cerre was now present; that I was ready to do justice to the world in general, by the punishment of Mr. Cerre, if he was found guilty of encouraging murder, or acquit him if innocent of the charge that they would give in their information. Cerre began to speak to them, but was ordered to desist. His accusers began to whisper to each other, and retire for private conversation; at length but one of six or seven were left in the room. I asked him what he had to say to the point in question. In fact I found that none of them had anything to say to the purpose. I gave them a suitable reprimand, and after some general conversation I informed Mr. Cerre that I was happy to find that he had so honorably acquitted himself of so black a charge; that he was now at liberty to dispose of himself and property as he pleased. If he chose to become a citizen of the Union, that it would give us pleasure; if not, he was at full liberty to dispose of himself. He made many acknowledgments, and concluded by saying that many doubts that he had were now cleared up to his satisfaction, and that now he wished to take the (*oath*) immediately. In short, he became a most valuable man to us. As simple as this may appear, it had great weight with the people, and was of infinite service to us, everything in this quarter having a most promising appearance.

Post Vincennes never being out of my mind, and from some things that I had learned I had some reasons to suspect that Mr. Gibault, the priest, was inclined to the American interest previous to our arrival in the country. He had great influence over the people at this period, and Post Vincennes was under his jurisdiction. I made no doubt of his integrity to us. I sent for him, and had a long conference with him on the subject of Post Vincennes. In answer to all my queries he informed me that he did not think it worth my while to cause any military preparation to be made at the falls of the Ohio for the attack of Post Vincennes, although the place was strong and a great number of Indians in its neighborhood, who, to his knowledge, were generally at war; that Governor Abbott had, a few weeks before, left the place on some business to Detroit; that he expected that when the inhabitants were fully acquainted with what had passed at the Illinois, and the present happiness of their friends, and made fully acquainted with the nature of the war, that their sentiments would greatly change; that he knew that his appearance there would have great weight, even among the savages; that if it was agreeable to me he would take this business on himself, and had no doubt of his being able to bring that place over to the American interest without my being at the trouble of marching against it; that his business being altogether spiritual, he wished that another person might be charged with the temporal part of the embassy, but that he would privately direct the whole, and he named Doctor Lafont as his associate.

This was perfectly agreeable to what I had been secretly aiming at for some days. The plan was immediately settled, and the two doctors, with their intended retinue, among whom I had a spy, set about preparing for their journey, and set out on the 14th of July, with an address and great numbers of letters from the French to the inhabitants, and letter to Mr. Gibault. Dr. Lafont's instructions are lost; Mr. Gibault, verbal instructions how to act in certain cases. It is mentioned here that Governor Abbott's letter to Mr. Rochblave had convinced us that they warmly adhered to the American cause, etc. This was altogether a piece of policy; no such thing had we known that they would, with propriety, suppose that Governor Abbott's letter to Rochblave had fallen into our hands, as he had written in that style respecting them, they most cordially verify it. Mr. Gibault was led to believe this, and authorizing them to garrison their own town themselves, which would convince them of the great confidence we put in them, etc.

All this had its desired effect. Mr. Gibault and his party arrived safe, and, after their spending a day or two in explaining matters to the people, they universally acceded to the proposal (except a few emissaries left by Mr. Abbott, who immediately left the country), and went in a body to the church, where the oath of allegiance was administered to them in the most solemn manner. An officer was elected, the fort immediately (*garrisoned*), and the American flag displayed, to the astonishment of the Indians, and everything settled far beyond our most sanguine hopes. The people here immediately began to put on a new face and to talk in a different style, and to act as perfect freemen. With a garrison of their own, with the United States at their elbow, their language to the Indians was immediately altered. They began as citizens of the state, and informed the Indians that their old father, the king of France, was come to life again, had joined the big knife, and was mad at them for fighting for the English; that they would advise them to make peace with the Americans as soon as they could, otherwise they might expect the land to be very bloody, etc. The Indians began to think seriously. Throughout the country this was now the kind of language they generally got from their ancient friends of the Wabash and Illinois.

Through the means of their correspondence spreading among the nations, our batteries now began to play in a proper channel. Mr. Gibault and party, accompanied by several gentlemen of Post Vincennes, returned to Kaskaskia about the first of August with the joyful news. During his absence on this business, which caused great anxiety in me (for without the possession of this post all our views would have been blasted), I was exceedingly engaged in regulating things in the Illinois. The reduction of these posts was the period of the enlistment of our troops.

I was at a great loss at this time to determine how to act and how far I might venture to strain my authority as my instructions were silent on many important points, as it was impossible to foresee the events that would take place. To abandon the country and all the prospects that opened to our views in the Indian department at this time, for the want of instructions in certain cases, I thought would amount to a reflection on government as having no confidence in me. I resolved to usurp all the authority necessary to carry my points. I had the greater part of our (*troops*) re-enlisted on a different establishment—appointed French officers in the country to command a company of the young inhabitants; established a garrison at Cahokia, commanded by Captain Bowman, and another at Kaskaskia commanded by Captain Williams, late lieutenant. Post Vincennes remained in the situation as mentioned. Colonel William Linn, who had accompanied us a volunteer, took charge of a party that was to be discharged on their arrival at the falls, and orders were sent for the removal of that post to the main land. Captain John Montgomery was dispatched to government with letters, and also conducted Mr. Rochblave thither.

The principles of the latter gentleman were so fixed and violent against the United (*States*) that (*his language*) was quite unsuitable. His lady had been (*allowed*) to take off all her furniture, etc., without (*opposition*) among the soldiers, except a few. The whole of her slaves were detained to be sold as plunder to the soldiers. which did not take place for some time—the officers generally wishing them to be returned to Mr. Rochblave (he being confined to his room in order to secure him from the soldiers, as he seemed to take a delight in insulting them on all occasions, and it was feared that some might do him a mischief), and were in hopes that the troops might be brought to conform to it, as many of them were men of substance, and the dividend would be but small and the credit would be considerable. This was in a fair way to take place, (*when*) some of the officers were desired to ask Mr. Rochblave to walk out and spend the evening at a certain house where a number of his acquaintances would be assembled. He did, but at the assembly he abused (*the officers*) in a most intolerable manner as rebels, etc. They immediately sent him off into the guard-house, and all further thoughts (*were abandoned*) of saving his slaves. (*They were*) sold and (*proceeds*) divided among (*the soldiers*), amounting to 1,500 pounds.

I informed the governor, by Captain Montgomery, of the whole of our proceedings and present prospects, pointing out the necessity of an immediate acquisition of troops, and that some person should be sent as head of the civil department, and referring him to Captain Montgomery for a general information of things.

This party being dispatched, I again turned my attention to St. Vincennes. I plainly saw that it would be highly necessary to have an American officer at that post. Captain Leonard Helm appeared calculated to answer my purpose. He was past the meridian of life and a good deal acquainted with the Indian (*disposition*). I sent him to command at that post, and also appointed him agent for Indian affairs in the department of the Wabash, as others were of this, in different quarters, expecting, by the fall, to receive information from the governor, when a strong garrison should be sent to him. He was fully possessed of my ideas and the plans I proposed to pursue, and about the middle of August he set out to take possession of his new command.

An Indian chief, called the Tobacco's Son, a Peankeshaw, at this time resided in a village adjoining St. Vincent. This man was called by the Indians "The Grand Door to the Wabash," as the great Pontiac had been to that of St. Joseph, and, as nothing of consequence was to be undertaken by the league on the Wabash without his assent, I discovered that to win him was an object of great importance. I sent him a spirited compliment by Mr. Gibault; he returned it. I now, by Captain Helm, touched him on the same spring that I had done the inhabitants, and the following speech, with a belt of wampum, directing Captain Helm how to manage, if the chief was peaceably inclined, or otherwise. The captain arrived safe at St. Vincent and was received with acclamations by the people. After the usual ceremony was over, he sent for the Grand Door and delivered my letter to him. After having it read, he informed the captain that he was happy to see him, one of the big knife chiefs, in this town—it was here that he had joined the English against him— but he confessed that he always thought that they looked gloomy; that as the contents of the letter was a matter of great moment, he could not give an answer for some time; that he must collect his counselors on the subject, and was in hopes the captain would be patient. In short, he put on all the courtly dignity that he was master of, and Captain Helm, following his example. it was several days before this business was finished, as the whole proceeding was very ceremonious. At length the captain was invited to the Indian council and informed by the Tobacco that they had maturely considered the case in hand and had got the nature of the war between the English and us explained to their satisfaction; that, as we spoke the same language, and (appeared to be) the same people, he always thought that he was in the dark as to the truth of it, but now the sky was cleared up; that he found that the big knife was in the right; that, perhaps, if the English conquered, they would serve them in the same manner that they intended to serve us; that his ideas were quite changed, and that he would tell all the red people on the Wabash to bloody the land no more for the English. He jumped up, struck his breast; called himself a man and a warrior; said that he was now a big knife, and took Captain Helm by the hand. His example was followed by all present, and the evening was spent in merriment. Thus ended this valuable negotiation and the saving of much blood.

This man proved a zealous friend to the day of his death, which happened two years after this, when he desired to be buried (*among*) the Americans. His body was conveyed to the garrison of Kohokia and buried with the honors of war. He appeared in all his conduct as if he had the American interest much at heart.

In a short time, almost the whole of the various tribes of the different nations on the Wabash, as high as the Ouiatenon, came to St. Vincennes and followed the example of their grand chief; and as expresses were continually passing between Captain Helm and myself the whole time of these treaties, the business was settled perfectly to my satisfaction, and greatly to the advantage of the public. The British interest daily lost ground in this quarter, and in a short time our influence reached the Indians on the river St. Joseph and the border of lake Michigan.

The French gentlemen, at the different posts that we now had possession of, engaged warmly in our interest. They appeared to vie with each other in promoting the business; and through the means of their correspondence, trading among the Indians, and otherwise, in a short time the Indians of the various tribes inhabiting the region of Illinois came in great numbers to Cahokia, in order to make treaties of peace with us. From the information they generally got from the French gentlemen (whom they implicitly believed) respecting us, they were truly alarmed; and, consequently, we were visited by the greater part of them without any invitation from us. Of course we had greatly the advantage, in making use of such language as suited our (*interest*). Those treaties that commenced about the last of August and continued between three and four weeks were probably conducted in a way different from any other known in America at that time. I had been always convinced that our general conduct with the Indians was wrong; that inviting them to treaties was construed by them in a different manner to what we expected, and implied, by them, to fear, and that giving them great presents confirmed it. I resolved to guard against this, and I took good pains to make myself acquainted fully with the French and Spanish methods of treating Indians, and with the manner and disposition of the Indians in general. As in this quarter they had not yet been spoiled by us, I

was resolved that they should not be. I began the business fully prepared, having copies of the British treaties.

After the great ceremony commonly made use of at the commencement of Indian treaties, the (*Indians*) as the solicitors opening it,
and after laying (*the*) whole blame of their taking up the bloody
hatchet to the delusion of the English, acknowledging their errors,
and many protestations of guarding in future against those bad birds
flying through the land (alluding to the British emissaries sent among
them), concluded in hoping that, as the Great Spirit had brought us
together for good, as He is good, that they might be received as our
friends, and that peace might take the place of the bloody belt—
throwing down and stamping on those emblems of war that they had
received from the British, such as red belts of wampum, flags, etc.

I informed them that I had paid attention to what they had said,
and that on the next day I would give them an answer, when I hoped
the ears and hearts of all people would be open to receive the truth
which should be spoken without deception. I advised them to keep
themselves prepared for the result of this day, on which, perhaps,
their very existence as a nation depended, etc., and dismissed them,
not suffering any of our people to shake hands with them, as peace
was not yet concluded—telling them it was time enough to give the
hand when the heart could be given also. They replied that "such
sentiments were like men who had but one heart, and did not speak
with a double tongue." The next day I delivered them the following speech:

Men an warriors! pay attention to my words. You informed me
yesterday that the Great Spirit had brought us together, and that you
hoped, as He was good, that it would be for good. I have also the
same hope, and expect that each party will strictly adhere to whatever
may be agreed upon—whether it be peace or war—and henceforth
prove ourselves worthy of the attention of the Great Spirit. I am a
man and a warrior—not a counselor. I carry war in my right hand,
and in my left, peace. I am sent by the great council of the big

knives, and their friends, to take possession of all the towns possessed by the English in this country, and to remain here watching the motions of the red people; to bloody the paths of those who attempt to stop the course of the river, but to clear the roads from us to those who desire to be in friendship with us, that the women and children may walk in them without meeting anything to strike their feet against. I am ordered to call upon the great fire for warriors enough to darken the land, and that the red people may hear no sound but of birds who live on blood. I know there is a mist before your eyes. I will dispel the clouds, that you may clearly see the cause of the war between the big knife and the English; that you may judge yourselves which party is in the right; and if you are warriors, as you profess to be, prove it by adhering faithfully to the party which you shall believe to be entitled to your friendship, and do not prove yourselves to be only old women.

The big knives are very much like the red people; they don't know how to make blankets and powder and clothes.

They buy these things from the English, from whom they are sprung. They live by making corn, hunting and trade, as you and your neighbors, the French, do. But the big knives, daily getting more numerous, like the trees in the woods, the land became poor and hunting scarce; and, having but little to trade with, the women began to cry at seeing their children naked, and tried to learn how to make clothes for themselves.

They soon made blankets for their husbands and children, and the men learned to make guns and powder. In this way we did not want to buy so much from the English. They then got mad with us, and sent strong garrisons through our country, as you see they have done among you on the lakes, and among the French. They would not let our women spin, nor our men make powder, nor let us trade with anybody else.

The English said we should buy everything from them; and, since we had got saucy, we should give two bucks for a blanket, which we

used to get for one; we should do as they pleased; and they killed
some of our people to make the rest fear them.

This is the truth and the real cause of the war between the English
and us, which did not take place for some time after this treatment.

But our women became cold and hungry and continued to cry.
Our young men got lost for want of counsel to put them in the right
path. The whole land was dark. The old men held down their
heads for shame because they could not see the sun, and thus there
was mourning for many years over the land. At last the Great Spirit
took pity on us, and kindled a great council fire, that never goes out,
at a place called Philadelphia. He then stuck down a post, but put a
war tomahawk by it, and went away. The sun immediately broke
out; the sky was blue again, and the old men held up their heads and
assembled at the fire. They took up the hatchet, sharpened it, and
put it into the hands of our young men, ordering them to strike the
English as long as they could find one on this side of the great waters.
The young men immediately struck the war post and blood was shed.
In this way the war began, and the English were driven from one
place to another until they got weak, and then they hired you red
people to fight for them. The Great Spirit got angry at this and
caused your old father, the French king, and other great nations, to
join the big knives and fight with them against all their enemies. So
the English have become like deer in the woods, and you may see
that it is the Great Spirit that has caused your waters to be troubled
because you have fought for the people he was mad with. If your
women and children should now cry, you must blame yourselves for
it, and not the big knives.

You can now judge who is in the right. I have already told you
who I am. Here is a bloody belt and a white one, take which you
please. Behave like men, and don't let your being surrounded by
the big knives cause you to take up the one belt with your hands,
while your hearts take up the other. If you take the bloody path,
you shall leave the town in safety and may go and join your friends,
the English. We will then try, like warriors, who can put the most

stumbling-blocks in each other's way, and keep our clothes long stained with blood. If, on the other hand, you should take the path of peace, and be received as brothers to the big knives, with their friends, the French, should you then listen to bad birds that may be flying through the land, you will no longer deserve to be counted as men, but as creatures with two tongues, that ought to be destroyed without listening to anything you might say. As I am convinced you never heard the truth before, I do not wish you to answer before you have taken time to counsel. We will, therefore, part this evening, and when the Great Spirit shall bring us together again, let us speak and think like men with but one heart and one tongue, etc., etc.

Whatever their private conversations on this subject might be, we never could learn, but on their return the next day the business commenced with more than usual ceremony. A new fire was kindled, all the gentlemen in town were collected, and, after all this preparatory ceremony was gone through, the chiefs, who were to speak, advanced near to the table where I sat with the belt of peace in his hand, another with the sacred pipe, and a third with the fire to kindle it, which was first presented to the heavens, then to the earth, and, completing a circle, it was presented to all the spirits—invoking them to witness what was about to be concluded—on to myself, and descending down to every person present.

The speaker then addressed himself to the Indians, the substance of which, was that they ought to be thankful that the Great Spirit had taken pity on them and had cleared the sky and opened their ears and hearts, so that they could hear and receive the truth, etc., etc. ; and, addressing himself to me, said that they had paid great attention to what the Great Spirit had put into my heart to say to them ; that they believed the whole to be the truth, as the big knives did not speak like any other people they had ever heard ; that they now plainly saw they had been deceived ; that the English had told them lies, and never had told them the truth, which some of their old men had always said, which they now believed ; that we were in the right, and as the English had forts in their country, they might, if they got strong, want to serve the red people as they did the big knives; that the red people ought to help us, and so forth; that they had, with a sincere heart, taken up the belt of peace and spurned the other away; that they were determined to hold it fast and would have no doubt of our friendship, as, judging from the manner of our speaking, that there was no room for suspicion; that they would call in all their warriors and cast the tomahawk into the river, where it could never be found again, and suffer no more emissaries, or bad birds, to pass through their land, to disquiet their women and children; that they might be always cheerful to smooth the roads for their brothers, the big knives, whenever they came to see them; that they would send to all their friends and let them know the good talk they had heard, and what was done, and advised them to listen to the same; that they hoped that I would send men among them, with my eyes, to see myself; they were men, and strictly adhered to all they had said at this great fire that the Good Spirit had kindled at Kohokias* for the good of all the people that would listen to it, etc.

This is the substance of their answer to me. The pipe was again kindled and presented to all the spirits to be witnesses; smoking of which, and shaking hands, concluded this grand piece of business, I suppose, with as much dignity and importance, in their eyes, as the treaty between France and America was to ours. They put on a different appearance; the greatest harmony now reigned, without the appearance of any distrust on their side, but we were not quite so tame, as I had set a resolution never to give them anything that should have the appearance of courting them, but generally made some excuse for the little I present them, such as their coming a long way to see me had expended their ammunition, wore out their leggings, or met with some misfortune or other; but they were generally alarmed, and the conclusion of peace satisfied them, and (we) parted, in all appearance, perfectly satisfied. I always made it a point to keep spies among them, and was pleased to find that the greatest of those

*Clark sometimes spells this Cahokia, Kohokia, Kohokias, and Cohos.

32

who treated with us strictly adhered to it, so that in a short time from this we could send a single soldier through any part of the Ouabash (*Wabash*) and Illinois country, for the whole of those Indians came to treat, either at Kohokias or St. Vincennes, in course of the fall.

It is not (*worth*) while (*to give*) the particulars of every treaty, as the one already mentioned conveys the idea of the plan we went on; the whole was held on the same principle, always sticking to the text, but varying in the manner of delivery to the different tribes—sometimes more severe, but never moderating except with those we were in friendship with. Of course (*to them*) a very different kind of a language was made use of. Their reply was nearly the same throughout the whole, and a boundary seemed now to be fixed between the British emissaries and our own at the heads of the waters of the lakes and those of the Mississippi, neither party caring much to venture too far. Some of the nations got divided among themselves, part for us, others for the English. Such a sudden change among the Indians in this region in our favor required great attention to keep up the flame from cooling, as the appearance of a reinforcement which we had reason to expect in the fall would ruin our influence. Every method was pursued to convince the French inhabitants that their interest, etc., was studied. Every restriction that they were formerly under that was disagreeable to them was done away. Their business with the commanding officers was done without fees—neither any at court, that sat weekly on their business—and many other little things, that (*had*) good effect; and, through them, our interest grew considerably among the French on the lakes, and many traders and others, watching their opportunities, came across with their goods and settled in the Illinois and St. Vincennes. This also had a good effect among the Indians. The friendly correspondence between the Spaniards and ourselves was much to our advantage, as everything the Indians heard from them was to our interest.

The behavior of two young men at the time of these treaties at Kohokias affected me very much, and (*it will*), perhaps, not (*be*) disagreeable to you to have their conduct related. A party of what

is called the Meadow Indians, who rove about among the different nations, composed partly of the whole of them, were informed that (*if*)
they would contrive to take me off they would get a great reward.
They came down, as others had done, some pretending to treat for
peace. They were lodged in the yard of Mr. Bradies, pretending
some acquaintance. About one hundred yards from my quarters, and
nearly the same distance fronting the fort, the little river Kohokias
passes (fronting the houses, on the opposite side of that part of the
street), which was then about knee deep. Having business at the time
with other Indians, they listened to what was passing, loitered about,
and got pretty well acquainted with our people. Having received
but a bad report of them, I took but passing little notice of them.
They had observed (*that*) the house I lodged in (*was*) very quiet
of nights, and supposed the guards to be but few (*and*) formed their
plan in the following manner: Some of them were to cross the
river, fire off their guns opposite to their quarters, on which they were
to attempt to get in, under the protection of the quarter guard, as flying from other Indians, their enemies, who had fired on them across
the river; if they succeeded, to butcher the guard and carry myself off.
A few nights after their arrival they made the attempt about one
o'clock. Having too much to think (*of*) to sleep much, I happened
to be awake at the time the alarm was given. They were immediately at the yard gate, when, the sentinel presenting his piece, being
a light night, they saw the guard paraded in front of the door more
numerous, perhaps, than they expected. They took a by-way and
got into their quarters.

The whole town was now under arms. The guard was positive it
was those Indians. They were immediately examined; said it was
their enemies had fired on them across the creek; that they wanted to
get under protection of the guard, but were not permitted, and made
the best of their way back to defend themselves; but some of the
French gentlemen, being better acquainted (*with*) them than the rest,
insisted that it was them—gave the alarm, sent for a candle and discovered that (*the*) leggings and moccasins of the fellows who had

crossed the river were quite wet and muddy. They were quite confounded—wanted to make various excuses—but (*were not*) suffered to speak. Their design was easily seen through. I said but little to them (and, as there were good many of other nations in town, and to convince the whole of the strict union of the French and us), I told them, as they had disturbed the town, the people might do as they pleased with them, and went away, but whispered that the chiefs should be sent to the guard-house and put in irons, which was immediately done by the inhabitants. They, in that situation, were every day brought into the council, but not suffered to speak, and, on finishing with the others, I had their irons taken off and told them that their designs were obvious to me, as a bird from their country had whispered me in the ear that all people said that they ought to die—which they must think themselves that they deserved, and what I intended—but, on considering the matter, and the meanness of the attempt to watch and catch a bear sleeping, I found that you were only old women and too mean to be killed by the big knives; but, as you ought to be punished for putting on British clothes like men, that shall be taken from you, and plenty of provisions given to (*take*) you home, as women don't know (*how*) to hunt, and as long as you stay here you shall be treated as all (*squaws*) ought to be; and, without any further notice of them, conversed indifferently with others present on very trifling subjects. They appeared to be much agitated. After some time they rose and advanced with a belt and pipe of peace, which (*they offered*) to me, and made a speech, which I would not suffer to be interpreted (at that time); and, a sword lying on the table, I broke their pipe and told them that the big knife never treated with women and for them to sit down and enjoy themselves as others did and not be afraid. What they had said was an acknowledgment of their design, excusing themselves by saying that it was owing to bad men that was among them from Michilimackinac that put it into their heads; that they were in hopes that we would take pity on their women and children; and, as their lives were spared when they deserved to lose them, they were in hopes that peace would be granted

them as it was to others, etc.   Several chiefs of other nations present
spoke in their favor, condemning their attempt; as they saw the big
knife was above little things, they wished I would take pity on the
families of those men and grant them peace, etc.   I told them that I
had never made war upon them ; that if the big knives came across such
people in the woods they commonly shot them down as they did
wolves, to prevent their eating the deer, but never talked about it, etc.

The conversation on the subject dropped.   For some time these
fellows continued busy in private conversation.   At last, two young
men advanced to the middle of the floor, sat down, and flung their
blankets over their heads.   This, at first, I did not (*know*) what to
make of.   Two of the chiefs, with a pipe, stood by them, and spoke
nearly in the same manner they had done before, and concluded by
saying that they had offered those two young men as an atonement
for things in general, and were in hopes that the big knives would be
reconciled after this sacrifice of them, etc., and again offered the
pipe, which I refused, and told them to go and sit down—that I would
have nothing to say to them—but in a milder tone than I had before
spoken to them.

It appeared that those people had got so completely alarmed
(which I had taken pains to do guarding desperation), that they supposed a tomahawk was hanging over the heads of every one of their
nation;   that nothing could save them but (*to*) get peace before
they left the place, and expected, by our putting to death or keeping
those two young men as slaves, that we should be reconciled.   The
young men kept their first position and frequently would push the
blanket aside, as if impatient to learn their fate.   I could have no
expectation of this business ending in this manner.   I always intended, at last, to be persuaded to grant those people peace, but this
astonished me.   I hardly knew whether it was sincere or not, but
everything proved it.   Every person present (there were a great number) seemed anxious to know what would be done, and a general
silence immediately took place.   For some time all (*was*) suspense.
I viewed those persons with pleasure.   You may easily guess at my

feelings on the occasion. I had read of something similar, but did not know whether to believe it or not, and never before, or since, felt myself so capable of speaking. I ordered the young men to rise and uncover themselves. I found there was a very visible alteration in their countenances which they appeared to try to conceal. I suitably harangued the whole assembly on the subject, and concluded by telling them I was happy to find there were men among their nation, as we were now witnesses there was at least two among those people. I then spoke to the young men—said a great (*deal*) in their praise—concluded by saying it was only such men as they that (*should be*) chiefs of a nation; that it was such that I liked to treat with; that through them, the big knives granted peace and friendship to their people; that I took them by the hand as my brothers, and chiefs of their nation, and I expected that all present would acknowledge them as such.

I first presented them to my own officers, to the French and Spanish gentlemen present, and, lastly, to the Indians, the whole greeting them as chiefs, and ended the business by having them saluted by the garrison. I wish I had a copy or could remember the whole I said on this business, but you may easily conceive from the nature of it. It appeared to give general satisfaction, but I thought the old chiefs appeared much cowed. Our new nabobs were now treated with great respect on all occasions.

A council was called in order to do some business with them, and great ceremony made use of, in order, more firmly, to rivet what had been done; and on the departure, some presents were given them to distribute among their friends at home, by whom I understood they were acknowledged and held in great esteem, and the Americans much spoken of among them. It would be difficult to account for the consequences, in case they had succeeded in their plan. It appears to have been but badly laid, but it (*was*) the worst problem they could have attempted in the town in daylight, and I never went out of it without guards too strong for them. The whole, as it turned out, was a fortunate adventure. It gave us much credit, and had good effect among the Indians in this quarter, as it soon became the subject of general conversation.

I now turned my attention to Saguina, Mr. Black Bird, and Nakionin, two chiefs of the bands of Sotaios and Outaway nations, bordering on Lake Michigan and the river St. Joseph. Mr. Black Bird and party were in St. Louis at the time Major Bowman took possession of Kohos, got alarmed and packed off, knowing that their nation was warmly engaged in the war, and not believing the Spanish protection sufficient to secure them against the revenge of the big knives who were so near at hand, although the governor persuaded them with a certainty of their being friendly received. Those chiefs, on their passage up the Illinois, met with numbers of traders (who had heard what had passed among their friends, and had already begun to alter their tone among the Indians) who persuaded them to turn back and see the big knives; for, as he had been so near them, and would not go to see them, they would think that he was afraid, and run away, etc. He excused himself by saying his family was sick, but that he would go in the spring; in the meantime would write to us. This letter I suppose he thought calculated to make us believe that they were friends to us, and I make no doubt but that their sentiments now daily changed in our favor. I made strict inquiry about Black Bird. I found that both were chiefs of considerable bands about St. Joseph, then at war; that Black Bird had great influence in that quarter, and it was thought by some traders lately arrived that he really wanted a conference, but wished to have an invitation, etc. I gave a man, who answered my purpose, two hundred dollars to visit him at St. Joseph, and wrote him a complete answer to his letter, inviting him to come (*to*) Kaskaskia that fall, which he did, with only eight attendants, and my messenger, Denoi.

After they had got rested and refreshed (*Black Bird*) observed some usual preparations making for an Indian council. He sent and informed me that he came to see me on business of consequence that concerned both our nations, and wished that we should not spend our time in ceremony; he said it was customary among all Indians, but that it was not necessary between us; that we could do our business sitting at a table much better; that he wanted much conversation with me, and hoped that there would be no ceremony used, etc. I found Mr. Black Bird of different manners to what others had been— that he assumed the airs of a polite gentleman, etc. A room was prepared and the nabob formally introduced by a French gentleman. After a few compliments he took his seat at one end of the table, myself at the other, the interpreters to our right and left; gentlemen seated around the room. Black Bird opened the conference, and attempted to speak as much in the European manner as possible. He said that he (*had*) long wished to have some conversation with a chief of our nation, but never before had an opportunity; he had conversed with prisoners, but he put little confidence in what they said, as they were generally afraid to speak; that he had engaged in the war for some time, but had always doubted the propriety of it, as the English and us appeared to be the same people. He was sensible that there was some mystery that he was unacquainted with; that he had only heard one side of the story, and now wished me to explain it to him fully, that he might be a judge himself, as he would then have heard both sides.

To satisfy this inquisitive Indian, I had to begin almost at the first settlement of America, and to go through almost the whole history of it to the present time, particularly the cause of the revolution; and as I must not speak to him as I did to other Indians, by similes, it took me near half a day to satisfy him. He asked a great number of questions very pertinent, and must be satisfied as to every point, which I was now more able to do, being pretty well acquainted with all the British officers had said to them.

He appeared to be quite satisfied, and said that he was convinced, from many circumstances, that what I had said was a true state of the matter; that he long suspected, from the conduct of the English, that they wished to keep the Indians in the dark, and it was now obvious to him; that he thought the Americans were perfectly right, and that they ought to be assisted than otherways; that he was happy to find that their old friends, the French, had joined us, and that the Indians ought to do likewise; but as I had said we would not wish it, they ought, at least, to sit still; that he would not blame us if we did as I had said, drive the whole off the face of the earth who would not do so, for it was plain to him that the English were afraid, otherways they would not give so many goods as they did for the Indians to fight for them; that he was perfectly satisfied, himself, that I might be assisted; that his sentiments were fixed in favor of us, and would no longer pay any attention to the English; that he would immediately put an end to the war, as to his part, but as many of their young men were then out, I must excuse that, but as soon as they returned he would make them lay down their arms, and not one of those that he influenced should again take them up; that on his return home he would take pains to tell the Indians, of every denomination, what had passed between us, and inform them of the true cause of the war, and that he was sure that the most of them would follow his example; that it would have good effect if I would send a young man among them, under his protection (which I did), as his appearance would give great might to what he himself said to them; that for the future he was in hopes we should view each other as friends, and that correspondence should be kept up between us, etc., etc.

I told him that I was happy to find that this business was likely to end so much to both our satisfaction, and so much to the advantage and tranquillity of each of our people; that I should immediately (*tell*) the governor of Virginia of what (*had*) passed between us, and that I knew that it would give him (*and*) all the Americans great pleasure, and that the Black Bird would be registered among their friends, etc., etc. Thus it was passed between us of a public nature.

After spending a few days with us he returned home. A young man of mine accompanied him. I had two pack horses loaded with necessaries for his journey home, and sent some presents to his family, perhaps to the amount of two or three pounds. Thus ended the business between this chief and myself, and as I had frequent opportunity of hearing from him, in the course of this fall, I found that he strictly adhered to what he had declared to me; that he had not only stopped his own tribe, but had great numbers of Indians in that quarter to (*become*) very cool in the British interest.

I had thought it policy in the course of all my conversation with the Indians to inform them that I did not blame them for receiving what presents the British chose to give them, but that it was degrading to them to make war as hirelings, etc.; that it was beneath the dignity of a warrior, etc.; the big knife views others who were at war against them, on their own account, with more (*favor*) than they did the hirelings; that the one was kept as great trophies, when, perhaps, the scalps of the others were given to the children to play with, or flung to the dogs. This kind of language, to a people we most ardently wished to be at peace with, may appear strange, but it had good effect among persons of their education, and perfectly consonant to our system of policy.

About this time, I received a letter from a chief named **Lajes**, or the Big Gate. It seems that this fellow, being a lad at the time Pontiac besieged Detroit, had shot a man standing in a gate, and immediately the name of Big Gate was given to him as a mark of honor. He had early engaged in the British interest and had led several parties against the frontier with good success, and on hearing what was going on in the Illinois, he fell in with some Pottawatimies on their way to see us, and came with them to hear what we had to say for ourselves. He had (*the*) assurance to make his appearance in a complete war dress, and the bloody belt that he had received from the English hanging about his neck; he attended the council for several days, always placed himself in front of the room and sat in great state, without saying a word to us, or we to him. I had found out (*what*) I wanted to know about him, and had fixed my resolutions, and in the course of my business with the other Indians, I had made use of several expressions in order to prepare my gentleman for what (*was to come*), and on the close of the business, I addressed myself to him. Told him I had been informed who he was, but, as he knew that public business must take place before private commences, I hoped that he would excuse me in (*not*) speaking to him before that time; that it was customary among the white people that when officers met in that manner, although enemies, they treated each other with greater respect than they did common people, and valued each other the more in proportion (*to*) exploits (*they*) had done against each other's nation. Especially as he had come designedly to see us, and business was now over, I hoped he would spend a few days more with us and that he would do us the pleasure of dining with the big knives that evening.

He appeared in nettles and rose and began to excuse himself. I would not hear, but ran on upon the same topic. I would stop; he would commence, and I would begin again, until I found I had worked him up to as high a pitch as I wished for, and then (*told*) him to go on. He stepped out into the middle of the floor, took off his belt of war and a small British flag that was in his bosom and flung them on the floor; then the whole of his clothes that he had on, except his breech cloth, struck his breast and addressed himself to the whole audience, and told them that they knew that he was a warrior from his youth, that he delighted in war, that the English had told him lies. He thought, from what they had said, that the big knives were in the wrong, and that he has been at war against them three times, and prepared to go again, but thought that he would rest himself a while and come here and see what sort of people we were and how (*we*) talked; that he had listened to everything that had been said; that he was now convinced that the English were wrong and that the big knives were right, and that he was a man and a warrior and would not fight in a wrong cause; struck his breast and said that he was now a big knife, and came and shook hands with me and the whole company as his brothers. A great deal of merriment ensued. The whole company appeared delighted in being merry. The fellow himself kept up their merriment by speaking to them as a new man and a big knife, but, as our new brother was now naked, it was necessary that he should be clothed, those that he had pulled off being pushed into the street by one of the servants. As we dispersed (*clothes were given him*), Captain McCarty having a suit a good deal laced. Captain Big Gate, at dinner, was much the finest man at table; and, to appear in as much state as the rest of us, he ordered some of his men to wait on him, but was rather awkward. As we had not suffered the Indians to dine with us, except chiefs of the greatest dignity, to prevent any jealousy pains were taken with those in town that were of as high rank as Mr. Lajes. After dinner was over he informed me that he wished to have some private conversation with me and pointed to a room that had a large window opening against a back street. Being always suspicious, I did not know but my new brother intended to stab me and make his escape through the window. I privately, unknown to him, made provisions against this, and we were shut up with the interpreter nearly half an hour. He gave me a history of himself and a full account of the situation of things at Detroit; said that he could do almost what he pleased at that place; if I chose it, he would go and bring me a scalp or a prisoner in forty days; as they did not know what had happened here, he could have what opportunity he pleased.

I told him that we never wished the Indians to fight for us; all we wished them to do was for them to sit still and look on; that those that would not might expect to be swallowed up, as they would see the lakes covered with boats belonging to the big knives, and wished he would by no means kill any person on our account, but that he would bring me news or a prisoner if he could get one handily; I should be glad, but by no means to hurt him. I gave him a captain's commission and a medal the day he took his departure, many Indians accompanying him.

As he took his leave at my quarters many gentlemen were present. They saluted him by firing their pistols through the window; passing in front of them, he was again saluted, which elated him much. He did not advance far before he stopped, and said he supposed those poor soldiers were hungry for a dram and ordered one of his men to go to a trader of his acquaintance, then in town, and get a little keg of rum and give it to them to drink his health, which was done; and they went off by water, up the Illinois river, where he fell in with some traders of his acquaintance who had got a permit at Mackinac to trade on those waters with a design to come to see us, and were then on their passage. Lajes asked them which way they were going; they said only trading. Then he asked them if they were not afraid of the big knives at Kohos. They said not. He then asked who they were. He said are you for the king of England, or the big knives? Knowing the fellow's character, they answered for the king of England, certainly. Was he not? He said no; that he was a captain of the big knives, and produced his commission, and told them they were enemies to his country, and his prisoners; that he would return and take them to his superior officer at Kohos. The men got alarmed; did not know what to make of the fellow, but found he was in earnest, and had a commission from under my hand and seal. They then told him that they were running away, and were going to the big knives. He said they were liars and would not believe them, and detained them for two or three days, until a party came by that he knew was in the American interest and became surety that they should deliver themselves up, and got a letter written to me dictated by himself. He warned the men to take care of themselves, for, if they were deceitful, and fell into his hands again, that he should treat them ill. This was a curious Indian letter. I can't remember the particulars of it further than it touched on the above business. It's lost with all the papers of the present year, except a few that, by chance, have been recovered.

Captain Big Gate proceeded on his journey, and, as long as I heard of him, behaved well; spoke much of his new dignity, abusing the other Indians for fighting as hirelings, etc., etc. Whether or not he ever after joined the (*British*), I never learned.

By this time, we had done business with almost all of the Indians on the Wabash and Illinois, and as high as the Ioways, Sauks and Renards, the inhabitants of the bottoms of Lake Michigan, etc., and the country at this time appeared to be in a perfect state of tranquillity. I was pleased to learn that our new post, at the falls of

Ohio, continued to gather strength, as well as the Kentucky in general, and that a powerful expedition was to move from Pittsburg to Detroit. This, with the thought of what we had done, caused us to enjoy ourselves for the first time since our arrival. But it did not last long. A party of the Missouri Indians came several hundred miles down that river to see us. Their curiosity was so great that they could not resist the temptation. They informed us that the whole of their business was a visit; that they had often heard of the big knives and wished to see them, and hoped that their curiosity (*might*) be excused, which was, and themselves and families treated (*well*) while they staid. They appeared to be something different in their manner, and complexion much fairer, than any other Indians I had seen, and suppose that that gave rise to the idea of there being Welch Indians in that quarter.

Captain Helm informed me, by express, that the British had sent an emissary to the (*Ouiatanon*) with considerable quantity of goods to attempt to regain the affections of the Indians in that quarter; that he thought he might be taken if I would authorize the attempt; several gentlemen at the Opost (*Vincennes*) were of the same opinion. I authorized the enterprise and empowed the captain to act agreeably to the councils held among themselves, but that if they, at any time, on finding the attempt dangerous or the chances against them, to relinquish the enterprise and return, giving out that they had only made a small excursion to see their friends, etc.

He set out by water with men, chiefly inhabitants of St. Vincent, and proceeded up the Wabash, the French merchants going along trading with the Indians on the way, and (*the*) captain speaking to (*them*) on public affairs as if this was intended as a visit he wished to pay them, and that those with him attended in compliance and to see a little about their trade. They did not appear as having any hostile intentions until they got near the Weaugh's. They then made all the expedition possible; entered the fort and took the Kite and twenty or thirty Chipeway warriors—then in council—prisoners. The emissary (I forget his name) frequently heard of this party coming up the river, but was told, by the Indians, that they meant no harm; that the big knives that were along only came with the traders to give good talks to his friends, etc. But after a few days he began to suspect the sincerity of the Indians and moved off up the river a little before Captain Helm arrived. Those Chipeways were a party he had invited to meet at the Weaugh and get supplied and make war at the Opost. They arrived but a few minutes before our party. Hearing the news and finding their friends gone, they stepped into the fort as a convenience to take some refreshments and hold a council. They had scarcely commenced before our party entered and closed the gate on them, as the inhabitants did not give them notice of the approach of the party. The Indians were much alarmed at finding themselves so suddenly taken, and had but little to say for themselves at first.

After some consultation between Captain Helm and the French gentlemen with him, it was thought that a good advantage might be made of this adventure, and fixed on the plan. There was a great deal said to the prisoners, but the whole amount was this: That the big knives never to catch a person stealing, and, as that was the case in the present instance, they, the Indians, were at liberty, and might fight for the English as long as they pleased; that if they again fell into the hands of the big knives, they might expect what would be their fate. The Indians gave a suitable answer to this seeming generosity, and declared that they would never fight against the big knives again, and I understand that these Indians frequently mentioned this adventure and spoke much in our favor.

Our party returned in safety to the Opost, having spoken with the greater part of the Indians, much to the satisfaction of both parties. So great was our interest among the Indians at this time, that Governor Hamilton, on his expedition against St. Vincent, with all his influence, could raise no more than four or five hundred Indians to accompany him.

The Chicasaws being at war, I wished to have some correspondence with them, to feel their pulse. I did not choose to send to them, as it would appear too much like begging a peace, as they call it. It occurred to me that the Kaskaskia Indians had been long at war with the Chicasaws, which had seemingly (*subsided*) for some time, and Batteast, the Kansas chief, I knew (*to be*) much in our interest. I proposed that he should go and propose a firm peace between him and the Chicasaws, and, if he succeeded, to mention something of the big knife. I was in hopes to bring on a correspondence in this manner. Batteast went without knowing what was my real design. The Chicasaws received him very kindly, but he could not complete his own business for the want of chiefs who were out of the way. He mentioned the Americans, but their conversation on the subject was cool and answered no good purpose.

The winter now approaching, things began to wear a more gloomy aspect. Not a word from government. Generally informed that there was a great preparation making at Detroit for a grand expedition and that some movement had already taken place as far as the Onitown (*Weatown*), and talks sent to all the Indians. We supposed that it was preparation to give the army from Fort Pitt as warm a reception as possible, etc.

All this information gave us, at first, some pleasure, until we learned that the army from Pittsburg, instead of marching into Detroit, had spent their time in parade and building a fine post to facilitate their future designs. This information we soon got from the falls and disappointed us very much.

One Denny, an inhabitant of Kohokia, was taken by Major Bowman for writing, through the Indians, to his friend near Detroit, giving dangerous information. His letters were intercepted, and himself tied to the tail of a cart, and by dawn received a lash at every door in town and (*was*) burned in the hand for other misdemeanors. This was the first and most severe punishment we had inflicted on any of the inhabitants. It was necessary at this time to show the people that we were capable of extremes either way, and that the good treatment we had shown them was from the principles of the government. No information from St. Vincent for some time past. As once a fortnight was the fixed time of the post, we began to suspect something was wrong. We sent spies that did not return, and we remained in a state of suspense. I had prepared to set out from Kaskaskia to Kohokia, but weather proved too bad for several days. At length set out, while it was snowing, but likely to clear up, which it did in about half hour. We observed that six or seven men had passed some distance on the road since the snow had ceased, which we supposed were persons from town, but wondered what they could be after. Having several chairs along (*and*) approaching near the river, one of the carriages sank into a rut. The gentleman who rode in it was some time getting it out, as the others would not suffer any assistance to be given until their laughter was out. We went cheerfully to Prairie de Rocher, twelve miles from Kaskaskia, where I intended to spend the evening at Captain Barber's. After supper a dance was proposed, in the height of which an express arrived, informing me that late that evening some negroes, being up the Kaskaskia river cutting of wood, that a party of white men and Indians came to them, and, after asking them a number of questions, told them that there were eight hundred of them lying within a few miles and they intended to attack the fort that night, but if they gave information they would be put to death, and went off. Some of the negroes gave the information, and the express dispatched after me. This sounded to us much like the truth.

We had had various suspicions for some time past; no information from the post, the various reports of the Indians, and our spies not returning, and the tracks we had seen in the road occurred to us. The village we were in was much alarmed. I was persuaded to cross the river to the Spanish side as a security of protection, as the fort must be invested before that time. I laughed at the idea, and, much to their amazement, resolved (*to make*) the attempt to get into the fort. I ordered our horses, borrowed clothes, and every man dressed like a hunter, and set out—politically making very merry on the subject. The snow was on the ground, and the moon shone very bright, taking the express with me in order to have time to think. In about

33

a quarter of an hour I wrote a card to Major Bowman, at Kohokia, ordering him down with his company and all the volunteers he could raise; to be cautious, and if he found that he could not render service, to make St. Genevieve his retreat, and to act [a word here doubtful]. The express was mounted on the best horse we had. Being an expert woodman, he had orders to run the horse as long as he could go faster than he could himself on foot, then to quit him and make the best of his way.

We proceeded, leaving the road where there was any woods for a covert for an enemy. The design of our dressing as woodmen, in leggins, cassocks, handkerchiefs tied on our heads, was, in case the enemy had actually invested the fort, to quit our horses, fall into their lines, and fight with the Indians, as probably they would not be apt to discover us from their friends, the English, until we could make our way good with them to a certain gut (*gully*), near one of the angles of the fort, where there was a small sally-port, where we could easily make ourselves known, and probably draw some of them into it. This was our plan. In seeming desperate situation, getting near the town, all was silent. We approached cautiously, discovered that no body of men had passed, as could be easily discovered in the snow. By our taking a circuitous route we were (*let*) in, much to the joy of the whole. I found every preparation I could have wished for, and, from every circumstance, we must expect the enemy in the neighborhood, particularly from the manner of the conversation with the negroes. The night passed off without any further alarm, and generally supposed that the snow had prevented the attack. I spent the night in various plans. I knew that it was impossible that we could defend the town or hold out long in the fort, but was in hopes of baffling the attempt, and fight them away. By a very plausible report (that they must have taken St. Vincent to get to us), we had received full information of their whole proceedings, and had sent an express to Kentucky for an army to march across and intercept their retreat, etc., etc.

As, by the report of the negroes, the most of the inhabitants of the town were much threatened, I was afraid that they would propose the defense of it, but, that nothing should appear wanting in us, I sent for the principal of them and put the question to them, and desired them to speak their sentiments freely. After some deliberation they told me that they thought it prudent to remain neutral. It was certainly a more judicious resolution and what I wished, but I made my advantage of it. I pretended to be in a passion, desired them to go to their homes, that I should do no further business with them, that I expected they would see their town in flames. They went off, and some of the young men came in volunteers. Some of them privately advised that all the wood in town be brought into the garrison, but received but a slight answer, and (*were*) told that we had plenty of provisions. Several buildings being near the walls of the fort, the inhabitants were told to move out, that they would be immediately burned. A large barn that stood not far off, full of grain, was immediately set on fire, without anything being taken out of it, and some other small buildings torn down and carried into the fort for fuel and preparations made to set other buildings on fire, for all was now confusion—the town on fire, the women and children screaming, moving, etc. I sensibly felt for them. Some of them begged to know how much of the town I intended to burn, that they might move their goods off. They were informed that it was far from us to destroy more than was absolutely necessary; that they must be sensible that, at a time like this, it was our duty to do anything necessary to promote our safety; that, although I knew the enemy would soon be intercepted by an army from Kentucky, yet they might do us much damage if we did not take necessary precautions; that we only meant to destroy the provisions, that it should not fall into the hands of the enemy; that they must confess that it was right; but the wind was unfavorable; no more buildings should be fired until it shifted.

They went off, and we waited to see the issue of this. In a very little time we observed the carts began to play, and in two hours we had upwards of six months' provisions in store. This policy was to make ourselves appear as daring as possible, as well as to get provisions. The people were desired to stop, as perhaps the report was false; that the spies would soon return, when we should know better how to proceed. They did, in a short time, and informed (*us*) that they had discovered the trail of seventy or eighty men, who appeared to direct their course towards the Opost, but no appearance of a formidable force in the neighborhood. Things got more quiet. The day following Major Bowman arrived with a considerable number of men. We now began to feel ourselves of more importance. It was now conjectured that St. Vincent was certainly in the hands of the enemy, and that the party (*who*) had been in the neighborhood had been sent from that place on some errand or other, and, the snow falling, found it impossible to remain undiscovered, as they must hunt; had given the alarm in order to have time to escape. This was nearly the case, as we hereafter learned. They were a party composed chiefly of Indians, sent by Governor Hamilton, then in possession of St. Vincent, with very polite instructions to lay in the neighborhood of the Illinois until they could get an opportunity of making a prisoner of me, but by no means to kill me; that, in case of success, they were to treat me with every politeness, on their return to furnish me with a horse, and to prevent me from taking a little amusement I should want on the way, but that I should be always attended by persons on better horses than I had myself. Thus I was to be a prisoner of state in the hands of the savages.

This party, by some means or other,—I never could be perfectly (*sure*) from whom (*they*) got information (*that*) a visit to the garrison of Kohokia (*was*) intended (*by me*). They fixed themselves back of a hill near the road, about three miles above Kaskaskia, always keeping a few as a lookout on the road. These fellows had advanced nearer to the town, the day I set out, than usual. The snow coming on, they had set out to return to their camp, and walked some distance in the road, which was the tracks we saw. The country in these parts being very open, and we riding very fast, they found it impossible to make their way good, so as to alarm their camp without being discovered, and secreted themselves behind some rocks and bushes, within seven or eight yards of the little gully, where the carriage swamped, and we tarried. They reported that they could have surprised and taken the most of us, but that not being able to distinguish me from the rest, as we were all muffled up with cloaks, they were afraid to fire for fear of killing me; but I imagine the truth was they were afraid to discover themselves, as (*we?*) were near double their number, and even the servants completely armed. The bad weather certainly (*helped?*), as they did not expect us out, and the body of them had returned to their camp, and only seven, who had advanced further on the road, were out.

Finding that their hopes were now blasted and that they could not remain without being discovered, they fell in with the negroes, with a design to raise such an alarm as should give them time to get off, which they completely effected. The instruction to this party was one principal cause of the respect shown to Governor Hamilton by our officers when he fell into our hands, but his treatment when he was in Virginia was very different and unsatisfactory to them, as they thought it in some measure affected themselves. But, to return, it was concluded to send other spies to St. Vincent, and in the meantime to prepare ourselves to act occasionally, being fully confident that a revolution would shortly take place, either for or against us. We wished to strengthen ourselves as much as possible. The volunteers who accompanied Major Bowman from Kohokia (*were*) dismissed, and an elegant set of colors presented to them. Those (*who were*) but badly armed were completed out of the stores, and presents made to the others, etc.

As an acknowledgment for the willingness they had shown on the present occasion, they paraded about town with their new flag and equipments, and viewed themselves as superior to the young fellow-Kaskaskians, which caused so much animosity between the two parties that it did not subside until I interfered some time after by a little piece of policy that reconciled them, while it suited my own convenience. After making every arrangement that we thought more conclusive to our safety, Major Bowman returned to his quarters, and we remained in suspense, waiting for the return of the spies. We had thought that if we found there was no probability of keeping possession of our posts to abandon them, just on the approach of the enemy, return to Kentucky, as that had considerably increased, raise a force sufficient to intercept and prevent the English from returning again to Detroit, as we knew the Indians were not fond of long campaigns and would leave them.

On the 29th of January, 1779, Mr. Francis Vigo, a Spanish merchant, who had been at St. Vincennes, arrived and gave the following information:

That Governor Hamilton, with thirty regulars, fifty French volunteers, Indian agents, interpreters, boatmen, etc., that amounted to a considerable number, and about four hundred Indians, had, in December last, taken that post, and as the season was so far advanced, it was thought impossible to reach the Illinois. He sent some of the Indians to Kentucky to watch the Ohio, disbanding of others, etc., the whole to meet again in spring, drive us out of the Illinois and attack the Kentucky settlements, in a body, joined by their southern friends; that all the goods were taken from the merchants of St. Vincent for the king's use; that the troops under Hamilton were repairing the fort, and expected a reinforcement from Detroit in the spring; that they appeared to have plenty of all kinds of stores; that they were strict in their discipline, but that he didn't believe they were under much apprehension of a visit, and believed that, if we could get there undiscovered, we might take the place. In short, we got every information from this gentleman that we could wish for, as he had had good opportunities, and had taken great pains to inform himself, with a design to give intelligence.

We now viewed ourselves in a very critical situation—in a manner cut off from any intercourse between us and the United States. We knew that Governor Hamilton, in the spring, by a junction of his northern and southern Indians, which he had prepared for, would be at the head of such a force that nothing in this quarter could withstand his arms; that Kentucky must immediately fall, and well if the desolation would end there.   If we could immediately make our way good to Kentucky, we were convinced that before we could raise a force even sufficient to save that country it would be too late, as all the men in it, joined by the troops we had, would not be sufficient, and to get timely succor from the interior frontiers was out of the question. We saw but one alternative, which was to attack the enemy in their quarters.   If we were fortunate, it would save the whole; if otherwise it would be nothing more than what would certainly be the consequence if we should not make the attempt.

Encouraged by the idea of the greatness of the consequences that would attend our success—the season of the year being also favorable—as the enemy could not suppose that we should be so mad as to attempt to march eighty leagues through a drowned country in the depths of winter; that they would be off their guard and probably would not think it worth while to keep out spies; that, probably, if we could make our way good, we might surprise them, and (*if*) we fell through, the country would not be in a worse situation than if we had not made the attempt.   These, and many other similar reasons, induced us to resolve to attempt the enterprise, which met with the approbation of every individual belonging to us.

Orders were immediately issued for preparations.   The whole country took fire at the alarm and every order was executed with cheerfulness by every description of the inhabitants—preparing provisions, encouraging volunteers, etc.—and, as we had plenty of stores, every man was completely rigged with what he could desire to withstand the coldest weather.

Knowing that the Wabash, at this season of the year, in (*all*) probability, would be overflowed to five or six miles wide, and to build vessels in the neighborhood of the enemy would be dangerous, to obviate this and to convey our artillery and stores, it was concluded to send a vessel round by water so strong that she might force her way, as she could not be attacked only by water, without she chose it, as the whole of the low lands was under water, and of course she might keep off any heights that were on the rivers.

A large Mississippi boat was immediately purchased and completely fitted out as a galley, mounting two four-pounders and four large swivels and forty-six men, commanded by Captain John Rogers. He set sail on the 4th of February, with orders to force his way up the Wabash as high as the mouth of White river, and to secrete himself until further orders, but if he found himself discovered to do the enemy all the harm he could without running too great a risk of losing his vessel, and not to leave the river until he was out of hope of our arrival by land; but, by all means, to conduct himself so as to give no suspicion of our approach by land. We had great dependence on this vessel. She was far superior to anything the enemy could fit out without building a new one, and, at the worst, if we were discovered, we could build a number of large pirogues, such as they possessed, to attend her, and with such a little fleet, perhaps, pester the enemy very much, and if we saw it our interest, force a landing. At any rate, it would be some time before they would be a match for us on the water.

As we had some time past been in a state of suspense, we had partly prepared for some such event as this. Of course, we were soon complete. The inhabitants of Kaskaskia, being a little cowed since the affair of the supposed intended siege, nothing was said to them on the subject of volunteers until the arrival of those (*from*) Kohokia, to whom an expensive entertainment, to which they invited all their acquaintances of Kaskaskias, all little differences made up, and by twelve o'clock the next day application was made to raise a company at Kaskaskia, which was granted and completed before night— the whole of the inhabitants exerting themselves in order to wipe off past coolness.

Everything being now ready, on the 5th of February, after receiving a lecture and absolution from the priest, etc., we crossed the Kaskaskia river with one hundred and seventy men; marched about three miles and encamped, where we lay until the 8th (refer to Major Bowman's journal for the particulars of this march), and set out, the weather wet, but, fortunately, not cold for the season, and a great part of the plains under water several inches deep. It was difficult and very fatiguing marching. My object now was to keep the men in spirits. I suffered them to shoot game on all occasions, and feast on it like Indian war-dancers—each company, by turns, inviting the others to their feasts—which was the case every night, as the company that was to give the feast was always supplied with horses to lay up a sufficient store of wild meat in the course of the day, myself and principal officers putting on the woodsmen, shouting now and then, and running as much through the mud and water as any of them. Thus, insensibly, without a murmur, were those men led on to the banks of the Little Wabash, which we reached on the 13th, through incredible difficulties, far surpassing anything that any of us had ever experienced. Frequently the diversions of the night wore off the thoughts of the preceding day. This place is called the two Little Wabashes. They are three miles apart, and from the heights of the one to that of the other, on the opposite shore, is five miles— the whole under water, generally about three feet deep, never under two, and frequently four.

We formed a camp on a height which we found on the bank of the river, and suffered our troops to amuse themselves. I viewed this sheet of water for some time with distrust, but, accusing myself of doubting, I immediately set to work, without holding any consultation about it, or suffering anybody else to do so in my presence, ordered a pirogue to be built immediately and acted as though crossing the water would be only a piece of diversion. As but few could work at the pirogue at a time, pains were taken to find diversion for the rest to keep them in high spirits, but the men were well prepared for this attempt, as they had frequently waded further in water, but, perhaps, seldom above half-leg deep. My anxiety to cross this place continually increased, as I saw that it would at once fling us into a situation of a forlorn hope, as all ideas of retreat would, in some measure, be done away with; that if the men began, after this was accomplished, to think seriously of what they had really suffered, that they prefer risking any seeming difficulty that might probably turn out favorable, than to attempt to retreat, when they would be certain of experiencing what they had already felt, and if (*the*) weather should but freeze, altogether impracticable, except the ice would bear them.

In the evening of the 14th, our vessel was finished, manned and sent to explore the drowned lands on the opposite side of the Little Wabash with private instructions what report to make, and, if possible, to find some spot of dry land. They found about half an acre and marked the trees from thence back to the camp, and made a very favorable report.

Fortunately the 15th happened to be a warm, moist day for the season. The channel of the river where we lay was about thirty yards wide. A scaffold was built on the opposite shore which was about three feet under water, and our baggage ferried across and put on it; our horses swam across and received their loads at the scaffold, by which time the troops were also brought across, and we began our march through the water. Our vessel (*was*) loaded with those who were sickly, and we moved on cheerfully, every moment expecting to see dry land, which was not discovered until (*we came*) to the little dry spot mentioned. This being a smaller branch than the other, the troops immediately crossed and marched on in the water, as usual, to gain and take possession of the nighest height they could discover. Our horses and baggage crossed as they had done at the former river, and proceeded on, following the marked trail of the troops. As tracks could not be seen in the water, the trees were marked.

By evening we found ourselves encamped on a pretty height in high spirits, each party laughing at the other in consequence of something that had happened in the course of this ferrying business, as they called it. A little antic drummer afforded them great diversion by floating on his drum, etc. All this was greatly encouraging, and they really began to think themselves superior to other men, and that neither the rivers nor the seasons could stop their progress. Their whole conversation now was concerning what they would do when they got about the enemy. They now began to view the main Wabash as a creek, and made no doubt but such men as they were could find a way across it. They wound themselves up to such a pitch that they soon took St. Vincent, divided the spoil, and before bedtime were far advanced on their route to Detroit.

All this was no doubt pleasing to those of us who had more serious thoughts. We were now, as it were, in the enemy's country—no possibility of a retreat if the enemy should discover and overpower us, except by the means of our galley, if we should fall in with her.

We were now convinced that the whole of the low country on the Wabash was drowned, and that the enemy could easily get to us, if they discovered us and wished to risk an action; if they did not, we made no doubt of crossing the river by some means or other. Supposing Captain Rogers had not got to his station, agreeable to his appointment, that we would, if possible, steal some vessels from houses opposite the town, etc. We flattered ourselves that all would be well, and marched on in high spirits.

On the 17th, dispatched Mr. Kennedy and three men off to cross the river Embarrass (this river is six miles from St. Vincennes), and, if possible, to get some vessels in the vicinity of the town, but principally if he could get some intelligence. He proceeded on, and getting to the river found that the country between that and the Wabash overflowed. We marched down below the mouth of the Embarrass, attempting, in vain, to get to the banks of the Wabash. Late in the night, finding a dog shot, we encamped, and were aroused, for the first time, by the morning gun from the garrison. We continued our march, and about two o'clock, 18th, gained the banks of the Wabash, three leagues below the town, where we encamped; dispatched four men across the river on a raft to find land, if possible, march to the town, if possible, and get some canoes. Captain W. McCarty with a few (men) set out privately the next (day) in a little canoe he had made, for the same purpose. Both parties returned without success. The first could not get to land, and the captain was driven back by the appearance of a camp. The canoe was immediately dispatched down the river to meet the galley, with orders to proceed day and night; but, determined to have every string to my bow I possibly could, I ordered canoes to be built in a private place, not yet out of hopes of our boat arriving—if she did, those canoes would augment our fleet; if she did not before they were ready they would answer our purpose without her.

Many of our volunteers began, for the first time, to despair. Some talked of returning, but my situation now was such that I was past all uneasiness. I laughed at them, without persuading or ordering them to desist from any such attempt, but told them that I should be glad they would go out and kill some deer. They went, confused with such conduct. My own troops I knew had no idea of abandoning an enterprise from the want of provisions, while there was plenty of good horses in their possession; and I knew that, without any violence, the volunteers could be detained for a few days, in the course of which time our fate would be known. I conducted myself in such a manner that caused the whole to believe that I had no doubt of success, which kept their spirits up.

This last day's march (February 21st) through the water was far superior to anything the Frenchmen had an idea of. They were backward in speaking, said that the nearest land to us was a small league called the sugar camp, on the bank of the river. A canoe was sent off and returned without finding that we could pass. I went in her myself and sounded the water; found it deep as to my neck.

I returned with a design to have the men transported on board the canoes to the sugar camp, which I knew would spend the whole day and ensuing night, as the vessels would pass but slowly through the bushes. The loss of so much time to men half starved was a matter of consequence. I would have given now a great deal for a day's provision or for one of our horses. I returned but slowly to the troops, giving myself time to think. On our arrival all ran to hear what was the report. Every eye was fixed on me. I unfortunately spoke in a serious manner to one of the officers. The whole were alarmed without knowing what I said. They ran from one to another, bewailing their situation. I viewed their confusion for about one minute, whispered to those near me to do as I did, immediately put some water in my hand, poured on powder, blackened my face, gave the warwhoop and marched into the water, without saying a word. The party gazed and fell in, one after another, without saying a word, like a flock of sheep. I ordered those near me to begin a favorite song of theirs. It soon passed through the line and the whole went on cheerfully.

I now intended to have them transported across the deepest part of the water, but when about waist deep one of the men informed me that he thought he felt a path—a path is very easily discovered under water by the feet. We examined and found it so, and concluded that it kept on the highest ground, which it did, and, by taking pains to follow it, we got to the sugar camp without the least difficulty (and what gave the alarm at the former proved fortunate), where there was about half an acre of dry ground, at least not under water, where we took up our lodging.

The Frenchmen we had taken on the river appeared to be uneasy at our situation. They begged that they might be permitted to go in the two canoes to town in the night. They said that they would bring from their own houses provisions without a possibility of any person knowing it; that some of our men should go with them, as a surety of their good conduct; that it was impossible that we could march from the place until the water fell; that (*would not be*) for a few days, for the plain, for upward of three miles, was covered two (*feet*) deep.

Some of the selected believed that it might be done. I would not suffer it. I never could well account for this piece of obstinacy and give satisfactory reasons to myself or anybody else why I denied a proposition apparently so easy to execute and of so much advantage, but something seemed to tell me that it should not be done, and it was not.

The most of the weather that we had on this march was moist and warm for the season. This was the coldest night we had. The ice, in the morning, was from one-half to three-quarters of an inch thick

near the shores and in still waters. The morning was the finest we
had on our march. A little after sunrise I lectured the whole. What
I said to them I forget, but it may be easily imagined by a person
who could possess my affections for them at that time. I concluded
by informing them that surmounting the plain, that was then in full
view, and reaching the opposite woods, would put an end to their
fatigue; that in a few hours they would have a sight of their long
wished for object, and immediately stepped into the water without
waiting for any reply. A huzza took place. We generally marched
through the water in a line; it was much easiest. Before a third
entered, I halted, and, further to prove the men, having some suspicion of three or four, I hallooed to Major Bowman, ordering him to
fall in the rear with twenty-five men and put to death any man who
refused to march, as we wished to have no such person among us.
The whole gave a cry of approbation that it was right, and on we
went. This was the most trying of all the difficulties we had experienced. I generally kept fifteen or twenty of the strongest men
next myself, and judging from my own feelings what must be that of
others. Getting about the middle of the plain, the water about knee
deep, I found myself sensibly failing, and as there were (*here*) no
trees nor bushes for the men to support themselves by, I doubted
that many of the most weak would be drowned. I ordered the
canoes to make the land, discharge their loading, and play backward
and forward, with all diligence, and pick up the men, and to encourage the party; sent some of the strongest men forward with orders
when they got to a certain distance to pass the word back that the
water was getting shallow, and when getting near the woods to cry
out "land." This stratagem had its desired effect. The men, encouraged by it, exerted themselves almost beyond their abilities—the
weak holding by the stronger, and frequently one with two others'
help, and this was of infinite advantage to the weak. The water
never got shallower, but continued deepening—even (*when*) getting to
the woods, where the men expected land. The water was up to my
shoulders, but gaining the woods was of great consequence. All the

low men, and the weakly, hung to the trees and floated on the old logs until they were taken off by the canoes. The strong and tall got ashore and built fires. Many would reach the shore, and fall with their bodies half in the water, not being able to support themselves without it.

This was a delightful, dry spot of ground, of about ten acres. We soon found that the fires answered no purpose, but that two strong men taking a weaker one by the arms was the only way to recover him, and, being a delightful day, it soon did. But fortunately, as if designed by Providence, a canoe of Indian squaws and children was coming up to town, and took through part of this plain as a nigh way. It was discovered by our canoes as they were out after the men. They gave chase and took the Indian canoe, on board of which was near half a quarter of a buffalo, some corn, tallow, kettles, etc. This was a grand prize and was invaluable. Broth was immediately made and served out to the most weakly with great care; most of the whole got a little, but a great many gave their part to the weakly, jocosely saying something cheering to their comrades. This little refreshment and fine weather, by the afternoon, gave new life to the whole.

Crossing a narrow, deep lake in the canoes and marching some distance, we came to a copse of timber called the Warrior's Island. We were now in full view of the fort and town, not a shrub between us, at about two miles' distance. Every man now feasted his eyes and forgot that he had suffered anything, saying that all that had passed was owing to good policy and nothing but what a man could bear, and that a soldier had no right to think, etc., passing from one extreme to another, which is common in such cases. It was now we had to display our abilities. The plain between us and the town was not a perfect level. The sunken grounds were covered with water full of ducks. We observed several men out on horseback, shooting of them, within a half mile of us, and sent out as many of our active young Frenchmen to decoy and take one of these men prisoner in such a manner as not to alarm the others, which they did. The information we got from this person was similar to that which we got from those we took on the river, except that of the British having that evening completed the wall of the fort, etc., and that there were a good many Indians in town.

Our situation was now truly critical—no possibility of retreating in case of defeat—and in full view of a town that had, at this time, upward of six hundred men in it, troops, inhabitants and Indians. The crew of the galley, though not fifty men, would have been now a reinforcement of immense magnitude to our little army (if I may so call it), but we would not think of them. We were now in the situation that I had labored to get ourselves in. The idea of being made prisoner was foreign to almost every man, as they expected nothing but torture from the savages if they fell into their hands. Our fate was now to be determined, probably in a few hours. We knew that nothing but the most daring conduct would insure success. I knew that a number of the inhabitants wished us well; that many were lukewarm to the interest of either; and I also learned that the grand chief, the Tobacco's Son, had, but a few days before, openly declared, in council with the British, that he was a brother and friend to the big knives. These were favorable circumstances, and as there was but little probability of our remaining until dark undiscovered, as great numbers of fowlers go out in the day, and that we now see and hear (*them*) through the plains around us, I determined to begin the career immediately, and wrote the following placard to the inhabitants and sent it off by the prisoner just taken, who was not permitted to see our numbers:

To the Inhabitants of Post Vincennes:

GENTLEMEN—Being now within two miles of your village with my army, determined to take your fort this night, and not being willing to surprise you, I take this method to request such of you as are true citizens and willing to enjoy the liberty I bring you, to remain still in your houses; and that those, if any there be, that are friends to the king of England, will instantly repair to the fort and join his troops and fight like men. And if any such as do not go to the fort should hereafter be discovered that did not repair to the garrison, they may depend on severe punishment. On the contrary, those who are true friends to liberty may expect to be well treated as such, and I once more request that they may keep out of the streets, for every person found under arms, on my arrival, will be treated as an enemy.

(Signed)   G. R. CLARK.

I had various ideas on the supposed results of this letter. I knew that it could do us no damage, but that it would cause the lukewarm to be decided, encourage our friends and astonish our enemies; that they would, of course, suppose our information good, and our forces so numerous that we were sure of success—and this was only a piece of parade; that the army was from Kentucky and not from the Illinois, as it would be thought quite impossible to march from thence, and that my name was only made use of. This they firmly believed until the next morning, when I was shown to them by a person in the fort who knew me well—or that we were a flying party that only made use of this stratagem to give ourselves (*a chance*) to retreat. This latter idea I knew would soon be done away with. Several gentlemen sent their compliments to their friends, under borrowed names, well known at St. Vincent, and the persons supposed to be at Kentucky. The soldiers all had instructions that their common conversation, when speaking of our numbers, should be such that a stranger overhearing must suppose that there were near one thousand of us.

We anxiously viewed this messenger until he entered the town, and in a few minutes could discover by our glasses some stir in every street that we could penetrate into, and great numbers running or riding out into the commons, we supposed to view us, which was the case. But what surprised us was, that nothing had yet happened that had the appearance of the garrison being alarmed—no drum nor gun.

We began to suppose that the information we got from our prisoners was false, and that the enemy already knew of us and were prepared. Every man had been impatient—the moment had now arrived. A little before sunset we moved and displayed ourselves in

34

full view of the town, crowds gazing at us.　We were flinging ourselves into certain destruction—or success; there was no midway
thought of.　We had but little to say to our men, except in calculat-
ing an idea of the necessity of obedience, etc.　We knew they did
not want encouraging, and that anything might be attempted with
them that was possible for such a number—perfectly cool, under
proper subordination, pleased with the prospect before them, and
much attached to their officers.　They all declared that they were
convinced that an implicit obedience to orders was the only thing that
would ensure success, and hoped that no mercy would be shown the
person who should violate them, but should be immediately put to
death.　Such language as this from soldiers to persons in our station
must have been exceedingly agreeable.　We moved on slowly in full
view of the town; but, as it was a point of some consequence to us
to make ourselves appear as formidable (*as possible*), we, in leaving
the covert that we were in, marched and countermarched in such a
manner that we appeared numerous.

In raising volunteers in the Illinois, every person who set about the
business had a set of colors given him, which they brought with them
to the amount of ten or twelve pairs.　These were displayed to the
best advantage; and as the low plain we marched through was not a
perfect level, but had frequent raisings in it seven or eight feet higher
than the common level, which was covered with water, and as these
raisings generally ran in an oblique direction to the town, we took the
advantage of one of them, marching through the water under it,
which completely prevented our men being numbered.　But our colors showed considerably above the heights, as they were fixed on long
poles procured for the purpose, and at a distance made no despica-
ble appearance; and as our young Frenchmen had, while we lay on
the Warrior's Island, decoyed and taken several fowlers, with their
horses, officers were mounted on these horses and rode about, more
completely to deceive the enemy.　In this manner we moved, and
directed our march in such a (*manner*) as to suffer it to be dark before we had advanced more than half way to the town.　We then

suddenly altered our direction, and crossed ponds where they could not have suspected us, and about eight o'clock gained the heights back of the town. As there was yet no hostile appearance, we were impatient to have the cause unriddled.

Lieutenant Bailey was ordered, with fourteen men, to march and fire on the fort. The main body moved in a different direction and took possession of the strongest part of the town. The firing now commenced on the fort, but they did not believe it was an enemy until one of their men was shot down through a port as he was lighting his match, as drunken Indians frequently saluted the fort after night. The drums now sounded and the business fairly commenced on both sides. Reinforcements were sent to the attack of the garrison, while other arrangements were making in town, etc.

We now found that the garrison had known nothing of us; that, having finished the fort that evening, they had amused themselves at different games, and had retired just before my letter arrived, as it was near roll-call. The placard being made public, many of the inhabitants were afraid to show themselves out of the houses for fear of giving offense, and not one dare give information.

Our friends flew to the commons and other convenient places to view the pleasing sight, which was observed from the garrison and the reason asked, but a satisfactory excuse was given; and, as a part of the town lay between our line of march and the garrison, we could not be seen by the sentinels on the walls. Captain W. Shannon and another being some time before taken prisoner by one of their (*raiding parties*) and that evening brought in, the party had discovered at the sugar camp some signs of us.

They supposed it to be a party of observation that intended to land on the height some distance below the town. Captain Lamothe was sent to intercept them. It was at him the people said they were looking when they were asked the reason of their unusual stir. Several suspected persons had been taken to the garrison. Among them was Mr. Moses Henry. Mrs. Henry went, under the pretense of carrying him provisions, and whispered him the news and what she had seen. Mr. Henry conveyed it to the rest of his fellow-prisoners, which gave them much pleasure, particularly Captain Helm, who amused himself very much during the siege, and, I believe, did much damage.

Ammunition was scarce with us, as the most of our stores had been put on board of the galley. Though her crew was but few, such a reinforcement to us at this period would have been invaluable in many instances. But, fortunately, at the time of its being reported that the whole of the goods in the town were to be taken for the king's use, for which the owners were to receive bills, Colonel Legras, Major Bosseron and others had buried the greatest part of their powder and ball. This was immediately produced, and we found ourselves well supplied by those gentlemen.

The Tobacco's Son being in town with a number of warriors, immediately mustered them, and let us know that he wished to join us, saying that by the morning he would have a hundred men. He received for answer that we thanked him for his friendly disposition, and, as we were sufficiently strong ourselves, we wished him to desist and that we would counsel on the subject in the morning; and, as we knew that there were a number of Indians in and near the town who were our enemies, some confusion might happen if our men should mix in the dark, but hoped that we might be favored with his counsel and company during the night, which was agreeable to him.

The garrison was now completely surrounded, and the firing continued without intermission, except about fifteen minutes a little before day until about nine o'clock the following morning. It was kept up by the whole of the troops—joined by a few of the young men of the town, who got permission—except fifty men kept as a reserve in case of casualty happening, which was many and diverting in the course of the night. I had made myself fully acquainted with the situation of the fort, town, and the parts relative to each. The gardens of St. Vincent were very near, and about two-thirds around it; the fencing of good pickets, well set, and about six feet high where those were watching. Breast-works were soon made by tearing down old houses, gardens, etc., so that those within had very little advantage to those without the fort, and not knowing the number of the enemy, thought themselves in a worse situation than they really were.

The cannons of the garrison were on the upper floors of strong block-houses, at each angle of the fort, eleven feet above the surface, and the ports so badly cut that many of our troops lay under the fire of them within twenty or thirty yards of the walls. They did no damage, except to the buildings of the town, some of which they much shattered, and their musketry, in the dark, employed against woodsmen covered by houses, palings, ditches, the banks of the river, etc., was but of little avail and did no damage to us, except wounding a man or two, and as we could not afford to lose men, great care was taken to preserve them sufficiently covered and to keep up a hot fire in order to intimidate the enemy as well as to destroy them. The embrasures of their cannons were frequently shut, for our riflemen, finding the true direction of them, would pour in such volleys when they were open that the men could not stand to the guns— seven or eight of them in a short time got cut down. Our troops would frequently abuse the enemy in order to aggravate them to open their ports and fire their cannons, that they might have the pleasure of cutting them down with their rifles, fifty of which, perhaps, would be leveled the moment the port flew open, and I believe that if they had stood at their artillery the greater part of them would have been destroyed in the course of the night, as the most of our men lay within thirty yards of the wall, and in a few hours were covered equally to those within the walls and much more experienced in that mode of fighting. The flash of our guns detected them, perhaps, the instant the man moved his body. The moment there was the least appearance at one of their loop-holes, there would probably be a dozen guns fired at it.

Sometimes an irregular fire, as hot as possible, was kept up from different directions for a few minutes, and then only a continual scattering fire at the ports as usual, and a great noise and laughter immediately commenced in different parts of the town by the reserved parties, as if they had only fired on the fort a few minutes for amusement, and as if those continually firing at the fort were only regularly relieved. Conduct similar to this kept the garrison eternally alarmed. They did not know what moment they might be stormed or [blown up?], as they could plainly discover that we had flung up some entrenchments across the streets, and appeared to be frequently very busy under the bank of the river, which was within thirty feet of the walls.

The situation of the magazine we knew well. Captain Bowman began some works in order to blow it up in case our artillery should arrive, but as we knew that we were daily liable to be overpowered by the numerous bands of Indians on the river, in case they had again joined the enemy (the certainty of which we were unacquainted with), we resolved to lose no time but to get the fort in our possession as soon as possible. If (*our*) vessel did not arrive before the ensuing night, we resolved to undermine the fort, and fixed on the spot and plan of executing this work, which we intended to commence the next day.

The Indians of different tribes that were inimical had left the town and neighborhood. Captain Lamothe continued to hover about it, in order, if possible, to make his way good into the fort. Parties attempted in vain to surprise him. A few of his party were taken, one of which was Maisonville, a famous Indian partisan. Two lads, who captured him, tied him to a post in the street, and fought from behind him as a breastwork—supposing that the enemy would not fire at them for fear of killing him, as he would alarm them by his voice. The lads were ordered, by an officer who discovered them at their amusement, to untie their prisoner and take him off to the guard, which they did, but were so inhuman as to take part of his scalp on the way. There happened to him no other damage. As almost the whole of the persons who were most active in the department of Detroit were either in the fort or with Captain Lamothe, I got extremely uneasy for fear that he would not fall into our power, knowing that he would go off if he could not get into the fort in the course of the night.

Finding that, without some unforeseen accident, the fort must inevitably be ours, and that a reinforcement of twenty men, although considerable to them, would not be of great moment to us in the present situation of affairs, and knowing that we had weakened them by killing or wounding many of their gunners, after some deliberation we concluded to risk the reinforcement in preference of his going again among the Indians. The garrison had at least a month's provisions, and if they could hold out, in the course of that time he might do us much damage. A little before day the troops were withdrawn from their positions about the fort, except a few parties of observation, and the firing totally ceased. Orders were given, in case of Lamotte's approach, not to alarm or fire on him without a certainty of killing or taking the whole. In less than a quarter of an hour he passed within ten feet of an officer and a party who lay concealed. Ladders were flung over to them, and as they mounted them our party shouted. Many of them fell from the top of the walls—some within and others back; but as they were not fired on they all got over, much to the joy of their friends, which was easily discovered by us; but, on considering the matter, they must have been convinced that it was a scheme of ours to let them in, and that we were so strong as to care but little about them or the manner of their getting into the garrison, our troops hallooing and diverting themselves at them while mounting, without firing at them, and being frequently told by our most blackguard soldiers of the scheme, and reason for suffering them to get into the fort—which on reflection they must have believed—but we knew that their knowledge of it could now do us no damage, but rather intimidate them. However, the garrison appeared much elated at the recovery of a valuable officer and party.

The firing immediately commenced on both sides with double vigor, and I believe that more noise could not have been made by the same number of men—their shouts could not be heard for the firearms; but a continual blaze was kept around the garrison, without much being done, until about daylight, when our troops were drawn off to posts prepared for them, from about sixty to a hundred yards from the garrison. A loophole then could scarcely be darkened but a rifle-ball would pass through it. To have stood to their cannon would have destroyed their men without a probability of doing much service. Our situation was nearly similar. It would have been imprudent in either party to have wasted their men, without some decisive stroke required it.

Thus the attack continued until about nine o'clock on the morning of the 24th. Learning that the two prisoners they had brought in the day before had a considerable number of letters with them, I supposed it an express that we expected about this time, which I knew to be of the greatest moment to us, as we had not received one since our arrival in the country; and, not being fully acquainted with the character of our enemy, we were doubtful that those papers might be destroyed, to prevent which I sent a flag, with a letter, demanding the garrison and desiring Governor Hamilton not to destroy them, with some threats of what I would do in case that he did if the garrison should fall into my hands. His answer was that they were not disposed to be awed into anything unbecoming British subjects.

The firing then commenced warmly for a considerable time, and we were obliged to be careful in preventing our men from exposing themselves too much, as they were now much animated, having been refreshed during the flag. They frequently mentioned their wishes to storm the place and put an end to the business at once. This would at this time have been a piece of rashness. Our troops got warm.

The firing was heavy, through every crack that could be discovered in any part of the fort, with cross shot. Several of the garrison got wounded, and no possibility of standing near the embrasures. Towards the evening a flag appeared, with the following proposition:*

*The proposition here referred to was not in this copy, but is inserted from Bowman's journal.

Governor Hamilton proposes to Colonel Clark a truce for three days, during which time he proposes there shall be no defensive work carried on in the garrison, on condition that Colonel Clark shall observe, on his part, a like cessation of any offensive work. That is, he wishes to confer with Colonel Clark as soon as can be, and promises, that, whatever may pass between these two and another person, mutually agreed upon to be present, shall remain secret till matters be finished, as he wishes that, whatever the result of their conference, it may be to the honor and credit of each party. If Colonel Clark makes a difficulty of coming into the fort, Lieutenant-Governor Hamilton will speak to him by the gate.

(Signed)   HENRY HAMILTON.
24th February, 1779.

I was greatly at a loss to conceive what reason Governor Hamilton could have for wishing a truce of three days on such terms as he proposed. Numbers said it was a scheme to get me into their possession. I had a different opinion and no idea of his possessing such sentiments, as an act of that kind would infallibly ruin him, but was convinced that he had some prospect of success, or otherways, of extricating himself. Although we had the greatest reason to expect a reinforcement in less than three days that would at once put an end to the siege, I yet did not think it prudent to agree to the proposals, and sent the following answer:

Colonel Clark's compliments to Governor Hamilton, and begs leave to inform him that he will not agree to any other terms than that of Mr. Hamilton surrendering himself and garrison prisoners at discretion. If Mr. Hamilton is desirous of a conference with Colonel Clark, he will meet him at the church, with Captain Helm, 24th February, 1779.   G. R. CLARK.

We met at the church, about eighty yards from the fort—Lieutenant-Governor Hamilton, Major Hay, superintendent of Indian affairs; Captain Helm, their prisoner; Major Bowman and myself. The conference began. Governor Hamilton produced articles of capitulation, signed, that contained various articles, one of which was that the garrison should be surrendered on their being permitted to go to Pensacola on parole. After deliberating on every article, I rejected the whole. He then wished that I would make some proposition. I told him that I had no other to make than what I had already made—that of his surrendering as prisoners at discretion. I said that his troops had behaved with spirit, that they could not suppose they would be worse treated in consequence of it, with their viewing us as savages; that if he chose to comply with the demand, though hard, perhaps the sooner the better; that it was in vain to make any proposition to me; that he, by this time, must be sensible that the garrison would fall; that both of us must [view?] that all blood spilled for the future by the garrison as murder; that my troops were already impatient, and called aloud for permission to tear down and storm the fort; if such a step was taken, many, of course, would be cut down, and the result of an enraged body of woodsmen breaking in must be obvious to him—it would be out of the power of an American officer to save a single man.

Various altercations took place for a considerable time. Captain Helm attempted to moderate our fixed determination. I told him he was a British prisoner, and it was doubtful whether or not he could, with propriety, speak on the subject. Governor Hamilton then said that Captain Helm was from that moment liberated, and might use his pleasure. I informed the captain that I would not receive him on such terms; that he must return to the garrison and await his fate. I then told Governor Hamilton that hostilities should not commence until fifteen minutes after the drums gave the alarm. We took our leave and parted but a few steps when the governor stopped, and, politely, asked me if I would be so kind as to give him my reasons for refusing the garrison on any other terms than those I had offered. I told him I had no objections in giving him my real reasons, which were simply these: That I knew the greater part of the principal Indian partisans of Detroit were with him; that I wanted an excuse to put them to death, or otherwise treat them, as I thought proper; that the cries of the widows and the fatherless on the frontiers, which they had occasioned, now required their blood from my hands, and that I did not choose to be so timorous as to disobey the absolute commands of their authority, which I looked upon to be next to divine; that I would rather lose fifty men than not to empower myself to execute this piece of business with propriety; that if he chose to risk the massacre of his garrison for their sakes, it was at his own pleasure, and that I might, perhaps, take it into my head to send for some of those widows to see it executed.

Major Hay paying great attention, I had observed a kind of distrust in his countenance, which, in a great measure, influenced my conversation during this time. On my concluding, "Pray, sir," said he, "who is that you call Indian partisans?" "Sir," I replied, "I take Major Hay to be one of the prinoipals." I never saw a man in the moment of execution so struck as he appeared to be—pale and trembling, scarcely able to stand. Governor Hamilton blushed, and, I observed, was much affected at his behavior in (*our*) presence! Major Bowman's countenance sufficiently explained his disdain for the one, and his sorrow for the other. I viewed the whole with such sentiments as I supposed natural to some men in such cases. Some moments elapsed without a word passing, as we could now form such disposition with our troops as render the fort almost useless. To deface that then could be no danger of course; supposed it prudent to let the British troops remain in the fort until the following morning. We should not have had (*such*) suspicions as to make so much precaution, but I must confess that we could not help doubting the honor of men whc could condescend to encourage the barbarity of the Indians, although almost every man had conceived a favorable opinion of Governor Hamilton. I believe what effected myself made some impression on the whole, and I was happy to find that he never deviated, while he staid with us, from that dignity of conduct that became an officer in his situation. The morning of the 25th approaching, arrangements were made for receiving the garrison (which consisted of seventy-nine men), and about ten o'clock it was delivered in form, and everything was immediately arranged to the best advantage on either side. From that moment my resolutions changed respecting Governor Hamilton's situation. I told him that we would return to our respective posts; that I would reconsider the matter, and that I would let him know the result. If we thought of making any further proposals (*than*) that of (*his*) surrendering at discretion, he should know it by the flag—if not, to be on his guard at a certain beat of the drum. No offensive measures should be taken in the meantime. Agreed to, and we parted.

What had passed being made known to our officers, it was agreed that we should moderate our resolutions. The following articles were sent to the garrison and an answer immediately returned:

In the course of the afternoon of the 24th the following articles (Major Bowman's MS. journal) were signed and the garrison capitulated:

1. Lieutenant-Governor Hamilton engages to deliver up to Colonel Clark Fort Sackville, as it is at present, with all the stores, etc.

2. The garrison are to deliver themselves as prisoners of war and march out, with their arms and accoutrements, etc.

3. The garrison to be delivered up at ten o'clock to-morrow.

4. Three days' time to be allowed the garrison to settle their accounts with the inhabitants and traders of this place.

5. The officers of the garrison to be allowed their necessary baggage, etc.

Signed at Post St. Vincent [Vincennes], 24th February, 1779.

Agreed, for the following reasons: The remoteness from succor, the state and quantity of provisions, etc.; unanimity of officers and men in its expediency, the honorable terms allowed, and, lastly, the confidence in a generous enemy.

(Signed)   HENRY HAMILTON,
                     Lieutenant-Governor and Superintendent.

The business being now nearly at an end, troops were posted in several strong houses around the garrison and patroled during the night to prevent any deception that might be attempted. The remainder, off duty, lay on their arms, and, for the first time for many days past, got some rest.

During the last conference a party of about twenty warriors who had been sent to the falls for scalps and prisoners, were discovered on their return, as they entered the plains near the town, and, there being no firing at this time, they had no suspicion of an enemy. Captain John Williams was ordered to meet and salute them. He went on, meeting them. The Indians supposed it a party of their friends coming to welcome them, gave the scalp and war-whoop and came on with all the parade of successful warriors. Williams did the same, approaching each nearer. The Indians fired a volley in the air; the captain did so, approaching within a few steps of each other; the chief stopped, as being suspicious; Captain Williams immediately seized him. The rest (*of the Indians*) saw the mistake and ran. Fifteen of them were killed and made prisoners. Two partisans and two prisoners were released and the Indians tomahawked by the soldiers and flung into the river.

We after this learned that but one of this party ever returned who got off, so that seventeen must have been destroyed. It was known by us that mostly the whole of them were badly wounded, but, as we yet had an enemy to contend with of more importance than they were, there was no time for pursuit, and (*spent*) but a few moments in executing the business before Captain Williams drew off his party and returned. Of course, the Indians who did not immediately fall, or were taken, got off.

One reason why we wished not to receive the garrison until the following morning was its being late in the evening before the capitulation was signed, and the number of prisoners that we should have, when compared to our own small force, we doubted the want of daylight to arrange matters to advantage, and we knew we could now prevent any misfortune happening.

On viewing the inside of the fort and stores, I was at first astonished at its being given up in the manner it was, but weighing every circumstance I found that it was prudent, and a lucky circumstance, and prob-

ably saved the lives of many men on both sides.   As the night passed
we intended to attempt undermining it, and I found it would have required diligence to have prevented our success.   If we had failed in
this, on further examination I found that our information was so good
that in all probability the first hot shot, after the arrival of our artillery, would have blown up the magazine, and would at once have
put an end to the business, as its situation and the quantity of powder
in it was such that it must have nearly destroyed a great part of the
garrison.   We yet found ourselves uneasy.   The number of prisoners
we had taken, added to those of the garrison, was so considerable
when compared to our own numbers, that we were at a loss how to
dispose of them so as not to interfere with our future operations.

Detroit opened full in our view—not more than eighty men in the
fort, great part of them invalids, and we found that a considerable
number of the principal inhabitants were disaffected to the British
cause.   The distance of any succor they could get, except the Indians, was very considerable.   The Indians on our route we knew
would now more than ever be cool towards the English ; that this
matter was never rightly considered by the continent—if it had, the
execution was but faintly attempted.   (*With*) possession of Detroit,
and a post of communication at Guihoga (*Cuyahoga ?*), supplies might
be always easily sent through that channel from Pittsburg, and Lake
Erie we might easily have in our possession, which would completely
put an end to all our troubles in this quarter, and perhaps open a door
to further advantageous operations.   Those were the ideas that influenced us at present.   We could now augment our forces in this quarter to about four hundred men, as near half the inhabitants of St. Vincent would join us.   Kentucky we knew could, perhaps, furnish immediately two hundred men, as there was a certainty of their receiving
a great addition of settlers in the spring ; with the addition of our
own stores, which we had learned were safe on their passage, added
to those of the British, there would not be a single article wanting for
such an attempt, and supplies of provisions might be got at Detroit.
For some time we privately resolved to embrace the object that

seemed to court my acceptance without delay, giving the enemy no time to recover from the present blows they had received, but wished it to become the object of the soldiery and the inhabitants before we should say anything about it; but it immediately became the common topic among them, and in a few days (*they*) had arranged things so that they were, in their imaginations, almost ready to march. They were discountenanced in such conversation, and such measures taken as tended to show that our ideas were foreign from such an attempt, but at the same time (*we*) were taking every step to pave our way. The great quantity of public goods brought from Detroit, added to the whole of those belonging to the traders of St. Vincent that had been taken, was very considerable. The whole was immediately divided among the soldiery, except some Indian medals that were kept in order to be altered for public use. The officers received nothing except a few articles of clothing they stood in need of. The soldiers got almost rich; others envied their good fortune, and wished that some enterprise might be undertaken to enable them to perform some exploit. Detroit was their object. The clamor had now got to a great height; to silence it and to answer other purposes they were told that an army was to march the ensuing summer from Pittsburg to take possession of Detroit, although from the last fall's proceedings we knew that no such thing was to be apprehended.

A complete company of volunteers from Detroit of Captain Lamothe's, mostly composed of young men, was drawn up, and when expecting to be sent off into a strange country, and probably never again returning to their connections, were told that we were happy to learn that many of them were torn from their fathers and mothers and (*sent*) on this expedition; others, ignorant of the true cause in contest, had engaged from a principle that actuates a great number of men—that of being fond of enterprise—but that they now had a good opportunity to make themselves fully acquainted with the nature of the war, which they might explain to their friends, and that, as we knew that sending them to the states, where they would be confined in a jail probably for the course of the war, would make a great number of our friends at Detroit unhappy, we had thought proper, for their sakes, to suffer them to return home, etc. A great deal was said to them on this subject. On the whole, they were discharged, on taking an oath not to bear arms against America until exchanged, and received an order for their arms, boats and provisions to return with. The boats were to be sold and (*proceeds*) divided among them when they got home. In a few days they set out, and, as we had spies who went among them as traders, we learned that they made great havoc to the British interest on their return, publicly saying that they had taken an oath not to fight against Americans, but they had not sworn not to fight (*for*) them, etc., and things were carried to such a height that the commanding officer thought it prudent not to take notice of anything that was said or done. Mrs. McComb, who kept a noted boarding-house, I understood, had the assurance to show them the stores she had provided for the Americans. This was the completion of our design in suffering the company to return. Many others that we could trust we suffered to enlist in the cause, so that our charge of prisoners was much reduced. Finding that ten boats loaded with goods and provisions were daily expected down the Wabash, and, for fear of the British who had them in charge getting intelligence and returning, on the 26th Captain Helm, Majors Bosseron and Legras, with fifty volunteers, were sent in three armed boats in pursuit of them.

On the 27th our galley arrived all safe, the crew much mortified, although they deserved great credit for their diligence. They had, on their passage, taken up William Myers, express from government. The dispatches gave much encouragement. Our own battalion was to be completed and an additional one to be expected in the course of the spring, but in the end proved unfortunate, and, on first reading, gave both pleasure and pain. We had but a day or two time to study on the subject, to fix on the plan of operation; that we were almost certain of success in case we without delay made the attempt on Detroit, as we knew our own strength and supplies, and wanted no farther information respecting that post; but, on the other hand, we were flattered with the prospect of an immediate reinforcement. A council was called on the subject.

I laid before the officers my plans for the immediate reduction of Detroit, and explained the almost certainty of success and the probability of keeping possession of it until we could receive succor from the states, which we might reasonably suppose they would make every exertion to furnish on receiving the intelligence which we could easily convey to them in a reasonable time. If we awaited the arrival of the troops mentioned in the dispatches (from the governor of Virginia), the enemy in the meantime might get strengthened, and probably we might not be so capable of carrying the (*post*) with the expected reinforcement as we should be with our present force, in case we were to make the attempt at this time; and in case we should be disappointed in the promised reinforcement, we might not be able to effect it at all. There were various arguments made use of on this delicate point. Every person seemed anxious to improve the present opportunity, but prudence appeared to forbid the execution, and induced us to wait for the reinforcement. The arguments that appeared to have the greatest weight were, that with such a force we might march boldly through the Indian nations; that it would make a great (*impression*) on them as well as the inhabitants of Detroit, and have a better effect than if we were now to slip off and take the place with so small a force, which was certainly in our power; that the British would not wish to weaken Niagara by sending any considerable reinforcements to Detroit; that it was more difficult for that post to get succor from Canada than it was for us to receive it from the states; that the garrison at Detroit would not be able to get a reinforcement in time to prevent our executing our designs, as we might, with propriety, expect ours in a few weeks. In short, the enterprise was deferred until the —— of June, when our troops were to rendezvous at Post Vincennes. In the meantime every preparation was to be made, procuring provisions, etc.; and, to blind our designs, the whole, except a small garrison, should march immediately to the Illinois; and orders were sent to Kentucky to prepare them-

35

selves to meet at the appointed time. This was now our **proposed plan**, and directed our operations the ensuing spring.

March 5th, Captain Helm, Majors Bosseron and Legras, returned from their journey up the river with great success. They came up with the enemy in the night, discerning their fires at a distance; waited until all was quiet; surrounded and took the whole prisoners, without the firing of a gun. Those (*British*) gentlemen were off their guard, and so little apprehensive of an enemy in that part of the world that they could hardly persuade themselves that what they saw and heard was real. This was a valuable (*prize*)—seven boats loaded with provisions and goods to a considerable amount. The provisions were taken for the public, and the goods divided among the whole, except about £800 worth (*of*) cloth (*for?*) the troops we expected to receive in a short time. This was very agreeable to the soldiers, as I told them that the state should pay them in money their proportion, and that they had great plenty of goods. This reservation was a valuable idea, for the troops, on their arrival, what few there were, (*were*) almost entirely naked.

On the 7th of March, Captains Williams and Rogers set out by water with a party of twenty-five men to conduct the British officers to Kentucky, and, farther to weaken the prisoners, eighteen privates were also sent. After their arrival at the falls of the Ohio, Captain Rogers had instructions to superintend their route to Williamsburg and be careful that all manner of supplies be furnished them on their way, and to await the orders of the governor.

Poor Myers, the express, got killed on his passage and his packet fell into the hands of the enemy, but I had been so much on my guard that there was not a sentence in it that could be of any disadvantage to us for the enemy to know, and there were private letters from soldiers to their friends, designedly written to deceive in case of such accidents. This was customary with us, as our expresses were frequently surprised. I sent a second dispatch to the governor, giving him a short but full account of what had passed and our views. The copy of this packet has been long since lost among many other papers, but I expect the original might be recovered among the public papers of those times.

I sent letters to the commandant of Kentucky directing him to give me a certain, but private, account of the number of men he could furnish me in June.

The weather being now very disagreeable, and having some leisure, our time was spent in consultation, weighing matters, and arranging things to the best advantage. A number of our men now got sick— their intrepidity and good success had, until this, kept up their spirits, but things falling off to little more than common garrison duty, they more sensibly felt the pains and other complaints that they had contracted during the severity of the late uncommon march, to which many of these valuable men fell a sacrifice, and few others were yet perfectly recovered (*from*) it.

I had yet sent no message to the Indian tribes, wishing to wait to see what effect all this would have on them. The Piankeshaws, being of the tribe of the Tobacco's Son, were always familiar with us. Part of the behavior of this grandee, as he viewed himself, was diverting enough. He had conceived such an inviolable attachment for Captain Helm, that on finding that the captain was a prisoner and not being as yet able to release him, he declared himself a prisoner also. He joined his brother, as he called Captain Helm, and continually kept with him, condoling their condition as prisoners in great distress, at the same time wanting nothing that was in the power of the garrison to furnish. Governor Hamilton, knowing the influence of Tobacco's Son, was extremely jealous of his behavior, and took every pains to gain him by presents, etc. When anything was presented to him, his reply would be, that it would serve him and his brother to live on. He would not enter into council, saying that he was a prisoner and had nothing to say, but was in hopes that when the grass grew, his brother, the big knife, would release him, and when he was free, he could talk, etc. Being presented with an elegant sword, he drew it, and, bending the point on the floor, very seriously said it would serve him and his brother to amuse themselves sticking frogs in the pond while in captivity. In short, they could do nothing with him, and the moment he heard of our arrival, he paraded all the warriors he had in his village (joining St. Vincent), and was ready to fall in and attack the fort, but for reasons formerly mentioned, was desired to desist.

On the 15th of March, 1779, a party of upper Piankeshaws and some Pottawattamie and Miami chiefs made their appearance, making great protestations of their attachment to the Americans, begged that they might be taken under the cover of our wings, and that the roads through the lands might be made straight and all the stumbling blocks removed, and that their friends, the neighboring nations, might also be considered in the same point of view. I well knew from what principle all this sprung, and, as I had Detroit now in my eye, it was my business to make a straight and clear road for myself to walk, without thinking much of their interest or anything else but that of opening the road in earnest—by flattery, deception or any other means that occurred. I told them that I was glad to see them and was happy to learn that most of the nations on the Wabash and Omi (*Maumee*) rivers had proved themselves to be men by adhering to the treaties they had made with the big knife last fall, except a few weak minds who had been deluded by the English to come to war; that I did not know exactly who they were, nor much cared, but understood they were a band chiefly composed of almost all the tribes (such people were to be found among all nations), but as these kind of people, who had the meanness to sell their country for a shirt, were not worthy of the attention of warriors, we would say no more about them and think on subjects more becoming us. I told them that I should let the great council of Americans know of their good behavior and knew that they would be counted as friends of the big knife, and would be always under their protection and their country secured to them, as the big knife had land enough and did not want any more; but if ever they broke their faith, the big knife would never again trust them, as they never hold friendship with a people who they find with two hearts; that they were witnesses of the calam-

ities the British had brought on their countries by their false assertions
and presents, which was a sufficient proof of their weakness; that
they saw that all their boasted valor was like to fall to the ground, and
they would not come out of the fort the other day to try to save the
Indians that they flattered to war and suffered to be killed in their
sight; and, as the nature of the war had been fully explained to them
last fall, they might clearly see that the Great Spirit would not suffer
it to be otherwise—that it was not only the case on the Wabash, but
everywhere else; that they might be assured that the nations who
would continue obstinately to believe the English would be driven out
of the land and their countries given to those who were more steady
friends to the Americans. I told them that I expected, for the future,
that if any of my people should be going to war through their country that they would be protected, which should be always the case
with their people when among us, and that mutual confidence should
continue to exist, etc., etc.

They replied that, from what they had seen and heard, they were
convinced that the Master of Life had a hand in all things; that their
people would rejoice on their return; that they would take pains to
diffuse what they had heard through all the nations, and made no
doubt of the good effect of it, etc., etc.; and, after a long speech in
the Indian style, calling all the spirits to be witnesses, they concluded
by renewing the chain of friendship, smoking the sacred pipe, ex-
changing belts, etc., and, I believe, went off really well pleased,
but not able to fathom the bottom of all they had heard, the greatest
part of which was mere political lies, for, the ensuing summer, Captain I. Shelby, with his own company only, lay for a considerable
time in the Wea town, in the heart of their country, and was treated
in the most friendly manner by all the natives that he saw, and was
frequently invited by them to join and plunder what was called "the
King's Pasture at Detroit." What they meant was to go and steal
horses from that settlement. About this time an express arrived from
the Illinois with a letter from Captain George.

Things now being pretty well arranged, Lieutenant Richard Brashear was appointed to the command of the garrison, which consisted of Lieutenants Bailey and Chapline, with one hundred picked men; Captain Leonard Helm commandant of the town, superintendent of Indian affairs, etc.; Moses Henry, Indian agent, and Patrick Kennedy, quartermaster. Giving necessary instructions to all persons I left in office, on the 20th of March, I set sail on board of our galley, which was now made perfectly complete, attended by five armed boats and seventy men.

The waters being very high, we soon reached the (*Mississippi?*),* and the winds favoring us, in a few days we arrived safely at Kaskaskia, to the great joy of our new friends, Captain George and company, waiting to receive us.

On our passage up the Mississippi, we had observed several Indian camps which appeared to us fresh, but had been left in great confusion. This we could not account for, but were now informed that a few days past a party of Delaware warriors came to town and appeared to be very impudent; that in the evening, having been drinking, they swore they had come there for scalps and would have them, and flashed a gun at the breast of an American woman present. A sergeant and party, that moment passing by the house, saw the confusion and rushed in. The Indians immediately fled. The sergeant pursued and killed (*some*) of them. A party was instantly sent to route their camps on the river. This was executed the day before we came up, which was the sign we had seen.

Part of the Delaware nation had settled a town at the forks of the White river, and hunted in the counties on the Ohio and Mississippi. They had, on our first arrival, hatched up a kind of peace with us, but I always knew they were for open war but never before could get a proper excuse for exterminating them from the country, which I knew they would be loth to leave; and that the other Indians wished them away, as they were great hunters and killed their game. A few days after this, Captain Helm informed me, by express, that a party of traders who were going by land to the falls were killed and plundered by the

* Copy says Missouri, but probably a mistake.

Delawares of White river, and that it appeared that their designs were altogether hostile, as they had received a belt from the great council of their nation. I was sorry for the loss of our men, otherwise pleased at what had happened, as it would give me an opportunity of showing the other Indians the horrid fate of those who would dare to make war on the big knives, and to excel them in barbarity I knew was, and is, the only way to make war and gain a name among the Indians. I immediately sent orders to St. Vincent to make war on the Delawares; to use every means in their power to destroy them; to show no kind of mercy to the men, but to spare the women and children. This order was executed without delay. Their camps were attacked in every quarter where they could be found; many fell, and others were brought to St. Vincent and put to death, the women and children secured, etc. They immediately applied for reconciliation, but were informed that I had ordered the war for reasons that were explained to them, and that they dare not lay down the tomahawk without permission from me, but that if the Indians were agreed, no more blood should be spilled until an express should go to Kaskaskia, which was immediately sent. I refused to make peace with the Delawares, and let them know that we never trusted those who had once violated their faith, but if they had a mind to be quiet, they might; and if they could get any of the neighboring Indians to be security for their good behavior, I would let them alone, but that I cared very little about it, etc., privately directing Captain Helm how to manage.

A council was called of all the Indians in the neighborhood; my answer was made public. The Piankeshaws took on themselves to answer for the future good conduct of the Delawares; and the Tobacco's Son, in a long speech, informed them of the baseness of their conduct, and how richly they had deserved the severe blow they had met with; that he had given them permission to settle that country, but not kill his friends; that they now saw the big knife had refused to make peace with them, but that he had become security for their good conduct, and that they might go and mind their hunting, and that if they ever did any more mischief— pointing to the sacred bow

that he held in his hand—which was as much as to say that he himself would for the future chastise them.   The bow is decorated with
beautiful feathers—an eagle's tail, and all the grandeur of the pipe of
peace, all the gaudy trinkets that can be put about it.   At one end is
a spear about six inches long, dipped in blood.   When Tobacco's
Son pointed the Delawares towards it, he touched it with his hand.
This bow is one of the most sacred emblems known to the Indians,
except the pipe of peace.   It is only allowed to be handled by chiefs
of the greatest dignity.

Thus ended the war between us and the Delawares in this quarter,
much to our advantage, as the nations about said that we were as
brave as the Indians, and not afraid to put an enemy to death.

June being the time for the rendezvous at (*Post Vincennes*), every
exertion was made in procuring provisions of every species, and
making other preparations.   I received an express from Kentucky,
wherein Colonel (*John*) Bowman informed me that he could furnish
three hundred good men.   We were now going on in high spirits,
and daily expecting troops down the Tennessee, when, on the ——,
we were surprised at the arrival of Colonel Montgomery with one
hundred and fifty men only, which was all we had a right to expect
from that quarter in a short time, as the recruiting business went on
but slowly, and, for the first time, we learned the fall of our paper
money.

Things immediately put on a different appearance.   We now
lamented that we did not march from St. Vincent to Detroit, but as
we had a prospect of a considerable reinforcement from Kentucky,
we yet flattered ourselves that something might be done—at least we
might maneuver in such a manner as to keep the enemy in hot water
and in suspense, and prevent their doing our frontiers much damage.
We went on procuring supplies and did not yet lose sight of our object, and, in order to feel the pulse of the enemy, I detached Major
Linetot, who had lately joined us, and a company of volunteers, up
the Illinois river under the pretense of visiting our friends.   He was
instructed to cross the country and call at the Wea towns, and then

proceed to Opost (*Post Vincennes*), making his observations on the route.   This, we expected, would perfectly cover our designs, and, if we saw it prudent, we might, on his return, proceed.   Early in June, Colonel Montgomery was dispatched, by water, with the whole of our stores.   Major (*Joseph*) Bowman marched the remainder of our troops by land.   Myself, with a party of horse, reached Opost in four days, where the whole safely arrived in a short time after.

Instead of three hundred men from Kentucky, there appeared about thirty volunteers, commanded by Captain McGary.   The loss of the expedition was too obvious to hesitate about it.   Colonel (*John*) Bowman had turned his attention against the Shawanee towns, and got repulsed and his men discouraged.

The business, from the start, had been so conducted as to make no disadvantageous impression on the enemy in case of a disappointment, as they could never know whether we really had a design on Detroit, or only a finesse to amuse them, which latter would appear probable.   Arranging things to the best advantage was now my principal study.   The troops were divided between St. Vincent, Kaskaskia, Cahokia and the falls of Ohio.   Colonel Montgomery was appointed to the command of the Illinois; Major Bowman to superintend the recruiting business—a number of officers were appointed to that service; Major Linetot and captains to superintend the Indian business, and myself to take up my quarters at the falls (*of the Ohio*) as the most convenient spot to have an eye over the whole.

Each person marching to his post in August, I arrived by land at the [manuscript torn] as far as White river in a few days.

Our movement during the summer had confused the enemy, consequently the commanding officers at Michilimackinac had sent an expedition, via St. Joseph, to penetrate the Illinois to drive the American traders out of it.   On their arrival at St. Joseph, while Major Linetot was on the way up the river, it was reported that an American army was approaching.   The Indians immediately fled from the English.   Being asked the occasion, (*the English were*) told that they were invited to see them and the big knives fight, and, as it was like to be the case, they had withdrawn to a height in order to have a full view of the engagement. Finding there was little dependence in the Indians, they withdrew to the mouth of the river St. Joseph and formed a strong camp, but on their first learning this intelligence they had sent an express to Mackinaw. A troop being dispatched off with provisions, and, coming within full view of their camp at the mouth of the river—supposing that it was the Americans, who had captured their friends at St. Joseph, and had taken post there. All the signs they could make could not bring the vessel to. She, returned with the disagreeable news, and the poor fellows had to starve until they could get an answer to a second express.

In the meantime, Mr. Linetot, knowing of all this, had changed his route to the Weaugh, which caused a conjecture that the whole body of us was directing our course to Detroit, which caused much confusion through the whole.

The summer was spent to advantage, as we were careful to spread such reports as suited our interest. I remained at Louisville until the spring following, continually discharging the multiplicity of business that was constantly brought from every quarter. I fully acquainted the governor of Virginia that, as the new settlers now peopling Kentucky were quite numerous, I was in hopes that they were fully able to withstand any force the enemy could send against her, and, perhaps, act on the offensive.

We now began to feel the effect of the depreciated state of the paper currency. Everything was at two or three prices, and scarcely to be had at any price. We set out on a plan of laying up, this fall, great quantities of jerked meat for the ensuing season, but as Detroit had pretty well recovered itself, the Shawanees, Delawares and other prominent Indian tribes were so exceedingly troublesome that our hunters had no success. Numbers being cut off, and small skirmishes in the country were so common that but little notice was taken of them. Colonel Rogers, who had been sent to the Mississippi for a very considerable quantity of goods, getting a reinforcement at the falls, on his passage to Pittsburg, a little above Licking creek, got

totally defeated; himself and almost the whole of his party, consisting of about seventy men, were killed or made prisoners. Among
the latter, of note, were Colonel John Campbell and Captain Abra-
ham Chapline. A small boat made her escape, which was all that
was saved.